THE

RESUME

HANDBOOK

THE RESUME HANDBOOK

How to Write Outstanding Resumes & Cover Letters for Every Situation

David V. Hizer & Arthur D. Rosenberg

Bob Adams, Inc.
Boston, Massachusetts

Published by
Bob Adams, Inc.
840 Summer Street
Boston, MA 02127

ISBN 0-937860-61-1

Manufactured in the United States of America

DEDICATION

The authors gratefully acknowledge the support and inspiration of Dave's wife, Sara, the contributions of Karen Baker and Hildegard Hizer, Dr. "H", who brought us together, and the editorial staff of Bob Adams, Inc..

TABLE OF CONTENTS

Preface

The *purpose* of a resume is *to obtain an interview.*

Your resume is your official representative, a verbal portrait calculated *to arouse an important person's interest in meeting you.*

Your resume is *not* an autobiographical profile. It isn't intended to make people like or admire you.

Think of it as a special tool with one specific purpose: *winning the interview.*

That's right, you've got to go out and *win* an interview, and only the inexperienced and the naive think otherwise. Your resume is the tool that gets your foot in the doors of the companies where you'd like to work. And if you don't get the interview, you won't get the job.

But there are other resumes out there in competition with your own. So yours must be at least as good as all the others if you're to stand an even chance. Of course, if yours is *better,* it may give you the advantage.

To write a winning resume, you must know *what* to say and *how* to say it. For this, you need *The Resume Handbook.*

Just as the purpose of your resume is *to obtain the interview,* the purpose of *The Resume Handbook* is to illustrate successful resume techniques.

The Resume Handbook tells you what kind of information to include in your resume, and what to leave out. Then it provides you with the tools and technique to present your chosen facts in a convincing and engaging manner.

The Resume Handbook will help you *win the interview*

The rest is up to you!

Introduction

After scrutinizing more than 10,000 resumes over a somewhat lesser period of years in professional recruiting work, a single, recurring impression looms large and dominant within our minds: *the overwhelming majority of resumes are overwhelmingly dull!*

Ah, but a veritable work of "art vitae" does happen by on rare occasion, one illuminated with a spark of true, creative thought, and which is pleasing to the eye. Now, if this isn't of itself enough to make our lives exciting, it may at least be interesting to read, and maybe — just perhaps — it will inspire sufficient curiosity to invite the author in for a closer look, which is of course the purpose of a resume.

The purpose of this book is to increase the minuscule percentage of superior resumes, in case we are obliged to read another 10,000 of them prior to retirement.

We've taken great pains to avoid the fat and wordy formats to which most books of this kind are prone. Instead, we've tried to heed our own advice on writing resumes by making our book interesting and to the point. *The Resume Handbook* presents the essential ingredients that go into successful resumes, with lucid explanations and the clearest of examples.

You can read it in less time than it takes to write a resume, then use it as a reference source when you are ready to begin writing your very own.

Included herein is a chapter on "The 25 Best Resumes We've Ever Seen." You will quickly learn what makes them so effective, and how to apply their winning techniques to your own purposes. The following chapter, "The 5 Worst Resumes We've Ever Seen," illustrates some of the pitfalls to be avoided at all costs, and may prove equally instructive.

The Resume Handbook focuses on three major objectives:

☐ *Organization:* How to structure and give visual impact to your resume so it immediately captures the reader's attention.

☐ *The Basic Principles:* What to include and what to leave out of your resume, to avoid wasting the reader's time and running the risk of turning him or her off.

☐ *Accomplishments:* How to write action-oriented accomplishments by using action verbs, enabling you to represent yourself as a highly-motivated achiever.

We have also included brief sections on cover letters and personal sales (also called *broadcast)* letters; they are too important to ignore, as they are an essential part of any job-hunting campaign. But our emphasis remains on writing resumes which will allow you to present yourself in the most appealing and engaging manner possible, to help you get the interviews you want.

—*Dave Hizer*
& Art Rosenberg

Chapter One:
Looking for a New Job

Nearly everyone looks for a job at some time in his or her life. The average American worker does so (according to the U.S. Bureau of Labor Statistics) every 3.6 years; according to the National Bureau of Economic Research, John and Jane Average work for 10 different employers during their respective lifetimes. In addition, four out of five job-hunters seek to *change careers* at least once.

It is estimated that over 40 million of our countrymen are currently involved in some sort of career change or transition. Approximately 33 percent of those now looking for a job are employed. Whether this is due to the economy, or the suggestion that a large portion of the work-force is under-utilized, the fact remains that competition in the job market is fierce.

Chin up, for all is not entirely bleak. The average firm, for instance, hires nearly as many new workers in a given year as its total number of employees. A construction company with 100 workers may have to hire as many as 200 per year, due to enormous turnover. Service firms with as few as 25 fulltime employees often need to hire 100 or more each year in order to maintain a stable staff.

So if you're looking for a job, you are in excellent company. Naturally, you need a system if you are to compete successfully, a technique which will give you the advantage. This is where *The Resume Handbook* can help, for whatever job search methods you may utilize, you'd better have a darned good resume to penetrate the screening process used by most employers.

WHAT IS A RESUME?

The only valid function of your resume is to get you invited for an interview. It is an advertisement of your skills, experience, and knowledge — presented in their most favorable light.

Your resume precedes you in your job search like an emissary of goodwill. Until you meet the interviewer (if you ever do), the resume is *all* they know of you. Approximately one interview is granted for every 245 resumes received. Obviously, a mediocre resume will rarely win an interview; a poor one hasn't got a chance!

Research tells us that a piece of advertising matter has about a second-and-a-half in which to attract the reader's interest. Someone sitting with a stack of 245 resumes (and probably a whole lot more) is simply not going to accord them equal time. So why not see to it that yours receives the lion's share of the interviewer's time?

Read on . . . we'll show you how.

WHY WRITE A RESUME IF I'M NOT LOOKING FOR A JOB?

Three reasons:

First, the majority of desirable positions are offered to individuals who are satisfied in their work and who are not necessarily seeking a new job. You never know when opportunity will knock, when the "job of a lifetime" may dangle within your grasp. Thus, it always pays to have an updated copy of your resume at hand for unexpected situations.

The second reason is that it can be a valuable experience to observe one's own professional career on paper. Your resume can help put your past experience, growth, and goals into perspective, to chart the path of your future career.

Finally, having a resume prepared can help protect you from the unexpected — losing your job in an economic turndown, for example. A well-prepared resume can take some of the anxiety out of the job search, especially for the experienced professional who suddenly finds him- or herself competing for jobs with young professionals who may be better versed in the latest job-hunting techniques.

RESUME ORGANIZATION

There are three commonly-used resume formats:

☐ *Chronological* resumes are safe for people with unbroken records of employment. It's a straightforward, easy-to-follow format (see resume examples 1, 4a, 6, 9, 12, 15, 19, 21, and 24 in "The 25 Best Resumes We've Ever Seen") which includes the dates of current and past employment.

☐ *Functional* (thematic) resumes, unlike chronological resumes, focus rather on accomplishments (see examples 2, 4b, 7, 10, 13, 16, 17, 20, and 22). This format is advisable for those with employment gaps due to unemployment or other activities they might prefer not to reveal (such as jobs from which they were fired or left after a short time, unsuccessful self-employment, prison terms, and a host of other reasons). It is also a better way to emphasize specific aspects of one's career. If, for example, you spent 11 years teaching engineering and only two years as an industrial engineer, a chronological resume would draw attention to your teaching background. But if you happened to be looking for an engineering position within a corporation, the functional format would allow you to play up your industrial experience and de-emphasize the academic side.

Another rationale for choosing the functional approach is if you haven't much to list by way of experience. This tends to be the case with recent graduates, individuals lately discharged from the armed services, and housewives seeking new (or planning to resume) careers after prolonged periods at home.

☐ *Combined* chronological/functional resumes can, when appropriate, offer the best of two worlds (see examples 3, 5, 8, 11, 14, 18, 23, and 25).

Each of these three resume styles will be demonstrated in intimate detail later in this book. But first:

RESUME PREPARATION

Composing even a brief autobiographical outline requires serious preparation and contemplation. So find a quiet spot (office, den, or diningroom table) where you feel comfortable and can be alone and undisturbed. Set aside a period of four to five hours, and if possible, unplug the phone.

Collect all the materials you will need, including:

● Pens, pencils, or both — whatever you like using best

● A lined pad (at least 8½" x 11")

● A good dictionary and a thesaurus

- Records of past employment, education, and related materials

- Copies of former job applications and correspondence, if available

- Descriptions of some jobs for which you plan to apply

- A copy of *The Resume Handbook*

These are the tools you'll need to prepare your resume. Now that you're suitably equipped, you can begin to formulate your own *resume strategy*. Be careful to observe the basic principles of resume-writing, which follow next.

Chapter Two:
The Basic Principles of Resume Writing

Writing a successful resume is an art form with certain basic principles that must always be kept in mind. The following suggestions have been formulated through long years of exposure to all sorts of resumes. Major deviations from these "rules" are at your own creative — and professional — risk.

☐ *Brief is Better!* Do not exceed two pages; see if you can fit it all on a single page (especially recent graduates and those early in their careers). Remember, few executives enjoy the task of reading piles of resumes, let alone the thick, voluminous monsters that get mailed out every day.

☐ *Format:* Your name (in bold type or in capital letters), address, and both home and work telephone numbers belong on top. Next come your objectives and summary of qualifications, employment history, education, and related activities and affiliations. Select a resume from "The 25 Best Resumes We've Ever Seen" which most closely meets your needs and suits your style, and use it as a model, or combine elements from several of these resume samples.

Education may precede employment history in certain cases, especially if a recent graduate or technical degree is more closely related to the desired position than your employment history. Recent graduates, with little or no work experience, have little choice.

☐ *Optional categories:* These may include career objectives, summary of qualifications, and such personal details as date of birth, marital status, military record, and health. Let's take a separate look at each of these:

● *Career Objectives:* This can be an excellent topic to include if you happen to possess a clear idea of what they are. But general or vague objectives are best omitted. Remember, your objectives can be honed specifically to the job for which you are applying in your *cover letter,* which we'll address a little later.

This optional category must be worded with precision if it is to be included on your resume. It should be clearly-stated and consistent with your accomplishments and demonstrated skills, as documented on your resume. Bear in mind the difference between "career" and "job" objectives. A *career* objective is just that . . . a long-range plan that may or may not relate directly to the job for which you are applying. A *job* objective, on the other hand, is oriented quite specifically to the job opening you wish to fill. We recommend using the term "objective" by itself, which would be appropriate for most situations.

● *Summary of Qualifications:* A detailed resume that includes a wealth of professional experience can effectively employ a "Summary of Qualifications." It may be inserted in addition to, or instead of, a statement of "Objectives;" or the two can be combined ("Qualifications and Objectives"). At its best, a "Summary" will entice the reader to read further; at its worst, it has the opposite effect. A summary is most helpful if the applicant has had an extremely diversified background, including (for instance) teaching and industry (see "The 25 Best"), or if the resume extends beyond a single page.

● *Personal Data:* If your personal details are "Mom-and-apple pie" and straight as the proverbial arrow, they may lend an air of respectability to your image. However, any non-essential information that you offer is more likely to work against you. Let's face it, prejudices *do* exist (for example) toward single women, unmarried men over a certain age, and older job-seekers — and why should *anyone* advertise that they're divorced? Your date of birth may only serve to persuade a potential employer that you are too young or too old for the job before they've even met you. Your military record may be worth mentioning if it includes some sort of relevant job training or experience (technical, organizational; see Abel Baker's resume in "The 25 Best"). And finally, who on earth would admit in writing to poor physical (or mental) health? Omit *any* reference to health.

☐ *Also leave out:*

● Reasons for having left a job — they won't enhance your image, and you may create a negative impression.

● Former (or desired) salary — you need to know as much as possible about the job in order to avoid asking for too little or too much. Don't risk putting yourself out of the running before you've even begun.

● Hobbies and memberships in social, fraternal, or religious organizations — potential employers don't need this information, and you never know what may turn them off.

● Reasons for *not* having served in the military.

- Any potentially negative information about you (unless unavoidable), such as prison terms, lawsuits lost, and handicaps that may affect your job performance.

- The label "Resume" or "Vitae" — if the briefest glance does not clearly identify your resume as such, the label will not help.

- The banal "References available on request;" this can be taken for granted, or you're out of luck.

☐ *Visual impact:* Vary type style; use bold type or italics to emphasize key words and subject headings (this will be discussed in chapter nine). If possible, select an off-white paper to help your resume stand out in a stack. Do not send out photocopies; spend a few dollars to have your resume professionally printed or word processed . . . the difference is well worth the cost. Make sure the resume is *letter-perfect.* Errors, typos, stains, abbreviations (*etc., e.g., i.e.),* technical jargon, and hip and buzz words are strictly taboo. Get your final draft critiqued and proofread by someone reliable.

☐ *Employment history:* Strike a balance between job content and accomplishments; the latter should be emphasized (as we'll explain in the next chapter). List your current position first, working back chronologically (unless you choose the less commonly-used functional or combined resume formats). Deemphasize the jobs you held further back in time. Avoid verifiable exaggerations that may someday constitute grounds for dismissal. Be sure to use action verbs and phrases (chapter three) to "polish up" the facts to your advantage.

An example of a balanced job history follows on the next page:

```
1979 to Present          Flinthall Electronics, Dover, Ohio.
                         Manager of product testing.  Supervise
                         testing group consisting of 7 research
                         engineers.  Group's mission was to create
                         methods to test performance, safety and
                         durability characteristics of projected
                         products.  While heading up this group:

                         * Initiated testing methods that
                           reduced annual budget of group
                           by 29%.

                         * Received award of excellence for
                           innovations in testing by American
                           Society of Research Engineers-1980.

                         * Increased group efficiency as
                           measured by time and quantity
                           parameters by 35%.

                         * Developed 3 patented testing pro-
                           cedures during last 4 years.
```

☐ *Organizations of which you are a member:* You may safely list the ones that show achievement or professional standing, such as the National Association of Certified Public Accountants, or the Tool & Die-maker's Guild. You can also indicate your leadership abilities as an officer or official in a strictly non-controversial association, like the PTA or Junior Achievement. But stay away from listing political, religious, and potentially controversial groups, because they simply don't belong on resumes.

☐ *Awards:* You should be sure to list awards that are relevant to the kind of job you're seeking, like Pulitzer Prizes, Oscars, or honorary doctorates. Leave out, however, any references to having won the league bowling, chess, or karate championship. While these achievements may bolster your ego, they make unwise assumptions about the interviewer. In addition, they have nothing to do with the task at hand — winning the interview.

□ □ □

With these basic resume strategy guidelines in mind, it's time now to focus on the specifics of making *your* resume stand out from the other 244.

Chapter Three:
Stating Your Accomplishments

The manner in which you state your accomplishments is no less important than the grim details themselves. Active, energetic phrases attract more of the reader's attention than do dull or passive words. "Created," for example, sounds more interesting than "began"; "promoted," "instituted," and "produced" are much more attention-getting than "worked on," "became," or "finished."

In fact, the very first word you use to describe an accomplishment can make the difference between an impressive resume and one that's just plain boring. It may also make the difference between its being read or "filed." So before presenting the mechanics of stating your accomplishments in their best possible light, let's pause to digest "Hizer's 57" — a list of action verbs that show you are an action *person,* the kind employers notice.

"HIZER'S 57"

ACTION VERBS

achieved	directed	organized
administered	eliminated	planned
advanced	established	prepared
advised	evaluated	produced
analyzed	expanded	promoted
authored	focused	provided
automated	headed up	published
coached	identified	reduced
conceptualized	implemented	researched
conducted	improved	restructured
contained	increased	reversed
contracted	initiated	saved
controlled	innovated	scheduled
coordinated	instituted	solved
created	introduced	streamlined
cut	led	supervised
decreased	maintained	taught
designed	managed	trained
developed	negotiated	trimmed

"Hizer's 57" is by no means a complete list of action verbs. They can, however, be applied to virtually any field or industry, actively demonstrating why your skills would be an asset to any employer. They also help to circumvent the danger of using buzz words, techno talk, and the like.

Now that you're armed with the right action *verbs,* it's easy to turn them into action *phrases* that best demonstrate your accomplishments.

ACTION PHRASES

Dull resumes tend to contain a lot of statements and descriptions that appear to have been copied directly from corporate personnel files. This, of course, is poor resume strategy. A better tactic is to employ phrases stressing your accomplishments in such a way as to attract — and hold — the reader's attention.

A winning resume contains a balance of job content and accomplishments. It also has attention-getting style. You may refer to this as "flair," "technique," or "pizzazz" . . . in *The Resume Handbook,* we call it *impact.*

To illustrate the point, here are some contrasting examples of statements often found in resumes. Those on the left are dull; in addition, they tell only half the story: *what was done.* The action phrases on the right, on the other hand, present a larger context in which to evaluate accomplishments more fully. And they are, indeed, more interesting to read, due in large measure to their effective use of action verbs.

Dull

With Impact

1. Raised level of sales above previous year.

1. Reversed negative sales trend; sales up 41% over prior year.

2. Started new employee programs that lowered turnover.

2. Created and implemented two new employee relations programs (flextime and job posting) that resulted in a 33% reduction in turnover.

3. Handled bookings for elderly pop group.

3. Managed bookings, travel, and accommodations for sexagenarian sextet.

4. Housewife of household with six people for past seven years.

4. Managed and organized six-member household with annual budget of $42,000.

5. Marketed new travel plan to corporations, increasing sales to $19 million.

5. Initiated new market concept of packaging travel to corporations for incentive programs, resulting in sales of $19 million (more than double expectation).

6. Worked for losing gubernatorial candidate for six months.

6. Organized and coordinated political campaign for leading gubernatorial candidate.

7. Opened new sales offices in two cities which broke quotas ahead of schedule.

7. Researched feasibility, then established two new sales offices; both operated above sales quotas within two years (six months ahead of schedule).

8. Hired and trained six new lion tamers during 1982-84. Only one serious casualty.

8. Recruited, trained, and motivated six new lion tamers during 1982-1984; five continue to excel.

9. Lowered operating costs in my division by $35,000.

9. Initiated cost-reducing plan in my division, resulting in 32% ($35,000) cost reduction with no negative effect on production capability.

10. Put on training sessions for supervisors in corporation.

10. Conducted leadership training for 48 supervisory/management level staff members.

11. Increased sales and profitability despite lower budget.

11. Expanded market penetration sales (by 14%), and profitability, during period of budgetary cutbacks.

12. Contributed to making group much more efficient.

12. Increased group efficiency, as measured by time and quantity parameters, by 35%.

13. Wrote ornithology procedures manual for museum.

13. Conceptualized and authored 88-page ornithology procedures manual for museum zoological research department.

In many of the preceding examples, you'll notice a relationship between the action verb used in the phrases with impact, and a more complete and detailed description of accomplishments. This is because action verbs *invite* further questions — even from *you* as you are reflecting on your achievements and writing your resume.

A careful blend of action verbs and specific accomplishments will get the interviewer's attention. It may also motivate him or her to call you in for a serious interview.

DESCRIBING YOUR EDUCATION

If your employment experience is limited, your educational background may be more relevant to the job you're seeking. In this case, your education will be the initial accomplishment you list (see examples in the next chapter). Regardless of whether it is your key accomplishment, or is subordinate to your job history, there are ways to present your educational background concisely and impressively.

For an individual with extensive employment experience, it is usually sufficient to list the bare details of your education:

1980 - B.S., Biology, Howard University, Washington, D.C.

or

Cornell University, Ithaca, N.Y.: M.B.A., Business Administration (1978)

or

Ball State University: Bachelor of Science, Molecular Chemistry, 1982.

You may, of course, list any academic honors earned:

1975 - San Diego State University, San Diego, California: M.A., History *(cum laude)*.

or

University of New Hampshire, 1984: B.A. in Fine Arts; graduated Summa Cum Laude.

If your employment experience is limited, it is a good idea to elaborate on educational achievements (before employment):

1983 - Bachelor of Arts Degree in Business Administration, University of Florida. Achieved 3.6 grade average (4.0 scale); specialized in management information systems. Senior project consisted of a 223-page report on the compatibility of selected information retrieval systems. Excerpts were published in July 1983 edition of *M.I.S.*

or

Boston University, School of Public Communication, 1977. Maintained 3.5/4.0 GPA; emphasized newspaper journalism sequence. While in school, served as editor of *The Daily Free Press* (1975-76); awarded John Scali Achievement Prize for best student investigative news story (1977).

If you have extensive relevant work experience in an academic setting (researchers, law students, journalism students, and many others), be sure to carefully describe that work with action phrases. Limited employment experience also necessitates creativity in describing other educational achievements. A lecture heard at college, at work, or on your own may be described as:

December 1982: Attended seminar on "Business Computer Languages" at RETI School of Electronics, Rapid City, SD.

or

Summer 1984: Participated in weeklong seminar on publishing procedures and marketing techniques, University of New Mexico.

List any relevant certificates you've earned:

Received "Fortran Programming Proficiency" certificate from ABC Business Institute, Phoenix, Arizona: February 1979.

or

Awarded certificate of proficiency in "Business Communication Machinery" from Control Info Institute, 1980.

If you lack a college degree, emphasize any classes attended or years completed. This can be worded so as to suggest you're in the process of completing a degree:

UNIVERSITY OF MIAMI (Evening Division): B.S., Mathematics; in progress.

or

Currently working on BS Degree in Public Administration, University of Delaware.

People with a lot of professional experience commonly list the seminars, lectures, or certificate programs they have attended, and so should you. This will help to mitigate any negative impressions your lack of a degree might create. Those who haven't earned college degrees are advised to list their high school diplomas. For example:

1968 - Diploma (with honors), Davis High School, Mt. Vernon, N.Y.

or

Graduated 1973 (college preparatory courses); Edgewater High School, Orlando, FL.

□ □ □

Following these guidelines on stating your accomplishments, your resume should fairly *sing* to an employer: *call me in for an interview; I can help your company.* Remember, your resume is all they know of you until you walk through that door for an interview. The only way an employer may identify you as an action-oriented individual is from your resume, and action verbs can help you to accomplish this objective.

Having mastered the art of using action verbs, your remaining task is a mechanical one: plugging in these action phrases into the following general format.

When stating your accomplishments, be sure to include:

● Name and location of the organization (city/ state only; street address is unnecessary)

- Specific job title

- Job description

- Skills applied

- Significant accomplishments

- Skills acquired (if applicable)

- Dates of employment (unless using functional format)

Focus on accomplishments that had a noticeable or measurable effect on some part of the establishment where you worked, such as:

- Sales increases, exceeding quotas, expectations, achievements vs. goals, winning recognition for the firm

- Organization/reorganization/innovation regarding staff, procedures, programs

- Development of new/innovative professional, management, or marketing strategies and products

- Projects for which you provided or contributed to leadership

- Positive results deriving from your actions/ proposals

In listing former jobs, it is recommended that you go back no more than 10-12 years, unless you've spent all that time with the same company; in that case, briefly list an earlier job or two.

Gaps in employment dates of more than a month or two should, if possible, be "hidden" (or satisfactorily explained: sabbatical to complete degree, illness, military service, etc.) by extending dates of earlier and later employment, or even better, by employing a functional format.

□ □ □

Once you've stated your accomplishments using action verbs and phrases that embellish your performance, you've completed the most difficult part of writing an effective resume.

Ready to begin? Before you do, we suggest you take a look at chapters four and five, to see how others have created their masterpieces . . . and disasters.

Chapter Four:
The 25 Best Resumes We've Ever Seen

The following resumes, appropriately edited and modified (in order to protect the authors), are among the best we've yet discovered. Selected from more than 10,000 resumes inspected over a period of years, these examples pull together the various techniques we've been discussing. Each one deals with a specific, real-life situation. The first, for instance, represents a successful and highly trained master chef who displays his talents with flair and charm; the fifth concerns a man about to leave the military; #10 portrays a graduating senior looking for his very first fulltime job; and #22 is for a housewife seeking to reenter the job market. There are examples here for just about every situation, and there are elements from each that you may want to consider incorporating into yours.

These 25 resumes are organized into the three categories we looked at earlier:

- *Chronological:* This type of resume is fairly straightforward, so we felt that nine examples would suffice (see resume examples 1, 4a, 6, 9, 12, 15, 19, 21, and 24).

- *Functional:* Many of our selected resumes fall into this category because it allows for a great deal of variation (see resume examples 2, 4b, 7, 10, 13, 16, 17, 20, and 22).

- *Combined:* Here we apply the best of both
  techniques (see resume examples 3, 5, 8, 11,
  14, 18, 23, and 25).

Good work speaks for itself, so we present these exemplary resumes intact. The concepts that make these resumes stand out are noted in the margins.

Each resume is labeled by format (chronological, functional, combined) and general background of the user. They are intended to serve as good examples of just about any career-oriented resume, and the lessons from each can be applied to your own uses.

Resume Example #1: An imaginative and creative "blue-collar professional" looking for a better job.

PIERRE CUISINE

MASTER CHEF

14 Fourchette Boulevard   Telephone (mornings)
New Orleans, Louisiana   (504) 544-0544

The proper blend of training and diversified
experience is my recipe for culinary excellence!

From the everyday to the extraordinaire, when
your clientele have tasted my international entrees
they will demand "encore".

CREATIVE OBJECTIVE
FOR A CREATIVE
BUSINESS.

EXPERIENCE
1981-   Arnaud's Restaurant   Head Chef
Present   New Orleans, Louisiana

Manage entire kitchen staff of 22 that produces the
finest luncheons and dinners in the South.
* Create extraordinary seafood, meat, and chicken
  dishes, specializing in delicate sauces.
* Supervise 3 assistant chefs and wine steward.
* Oversee training of 4 apprentices.
* Responsible for purchases of all foods.

EVIDENCE OF
MANAGEMENT
ABILITIES AND
EXPERIENCE.

1976-   Le Chateau   Chef
1981   Charlesbourg, Quebec

One of 2 chefs directly under head chef.
* Prepared special sauces and such delicate
  specialties as pheasant-under-glass.
* Served flambees and other spectacular dishes in
  dining room.

1972-   Chez Paul Beaucoup   Apprentice Chef
1976   Paris, France

* Prepared hors d'oeuvres, entrees and desserts under
  the direction of one of the world's foremost chefs.
* Assisted in the purchase of foods and kitchen supplies.

THE TYPE OF TRAINING
THAT STANDS OUT.

EDUCATION
1971   Diploma, Ecole d'Haute Cuisine, Lyons, France.
                   Generally recognized as the leading cooking school in
                   Europe.

MAKES AN IMPORTANT
POINT THAT MIGHT
OTHERWISE BE
OVERLOOKED.

SPECIAL TALENTS
                   * Capable of serving as knowledgeable wine steward.
                   * Fluent French and English; spoken Italian and Spanish.
                   * Aware of kosher dietary laws.

PERSONAL   Dual Nationality: French and Canadian.
                   Willing to relocate anywhere in the world.

CLEVER, WITTY,
APPEALING.

CHRONOLOGICAL

49

Resume Example #2: Unemployed, but with solid office skills and a record of steady employment.

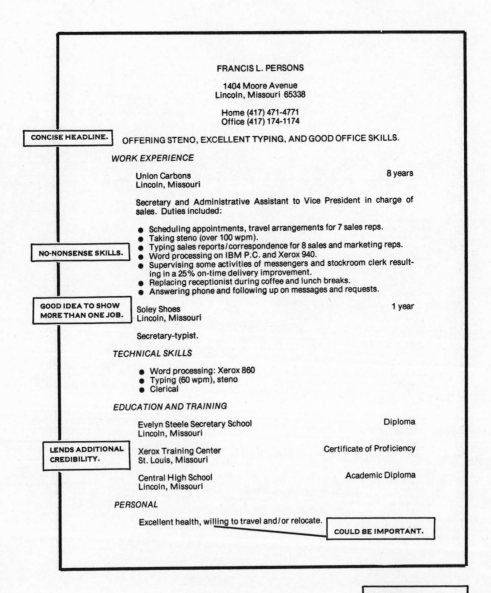

FRANCIS L. PERSONS

1404 Moore Avenue
Lincoln, Missouri 65338

Home (417) 471-4771
Office (417) 174-1174

CONCISE HEADLINE.

OFFERING STENO, EXCELLENT TYPING, AND GOOD OFFICE SKILLS.

WORK EXPERIENCE

Union Carbons   8 years
Lincoln, Missouri

Secretary and Administrative Assistant to Vice President in charge of sales. Duties included:

NO-NONSENSE SKILLS.

- Scheduling appointments, travel arrangements for 7 sales reps.
- Taking steno (over 100 wpm).
- Typing sales reports/correspondence for 8 sales and marketing reps.
- Word processing on IBM P.C. and Xerox 940.
- Supervising some activities of messengers and stockroom clerk resulting in a 25% on-time delivery improvement.
- Replacing receptionist during coffee and lunch breaks.
- Answering phone and following up on messages and requests.

GOOD IDEA TO SHOW MORE THAN ONE JOB.

Soley Shoes   1 year
Lincoln, Missouri

Secretary-typist.

TECHNICAL SKILLS

- Word processing: Xerox 860
- Typing (60 wpm), steno
- Clerical

EDUCATION AND TRAINING

Evelyn Steele Secretary School   Diploma
Lincoln, Missouri

LENDS ADDITIONAL CREDIBILITY.

Xerox Training Center   Certificate of Proficiency
St. Louis, Missouri

Central High School   Academic Diploma
Lincoln, Missouri

PERSONAL

Excellent health, willing to travel and/or relocate.

COULD BE IMPORTANT.

FUNCTIONAL

A NO-FRILLS, BUSINESSLIKE APPROACH TO LOOKING FOR A JOB.

Resume Example #3: High-tech!

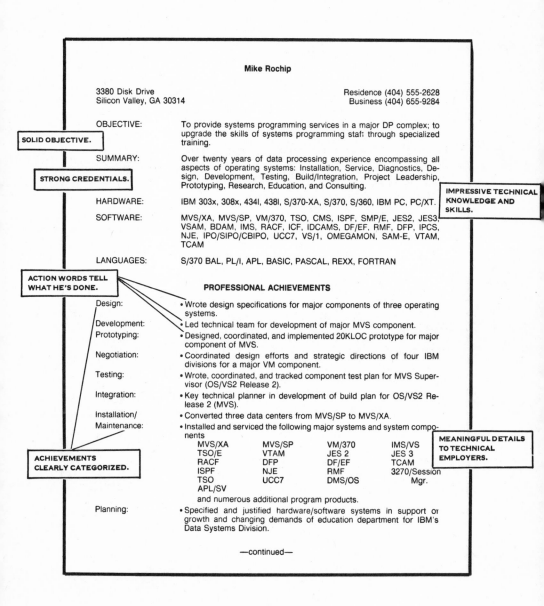

Mike Rochip

3380 Disk Drive
Silicon Valley, GA 30314

Residence (404) 555-2628
Business (404) 655-9284

OBJECTIVE: To provide systems programming services in a major DP complex; to upgrade the skills of systems programming staff through specialized training.

SOLID OBJECTIVE.

SUMMARY: Over twenty years of data processing experience encompassing all aspects of operating systems: Installation, Service, Diagnostics, Design, Development, Testing, Build/Integration, Project Leadership, Prototyping, Research, Education, and Consulting.

STRONG CREDENTIALS.

HARDWARE: IBM 303x, 308x, 434I, 438I, S/370-XA, S/370, S/360, IBM PC, PC/XT.

IMPRESSIVE TECHNICAL KNOWLEDGE AND SKILLS.

SOFTWARE: MVS/XA, MVS/SP, VM/370, TSO, CMS, ISPF, SMP/E, JES2, JES3, VSAM, BDAM, IMS, RACF, ICF, IDCAMS, DF/EF, RMF, DFP, IPCS, NJE, IPO/SIPO/CBIPO, UCC7, VS/1, OMEGAMON, SAM-E, VTAM, TCAM

LANGUAGES: S/370 BAL, PL/I, APL, BASIC, PASCAL, REXX, FORTRAN

ACTION WORDS TELL WHAT HE'S DONE.

PROFESSIONAL ACHIEVEMENTS

Design:
- Wrote design specifications for major components of three operating systems.

Development:
- Led technical team for development of major MVS component.

Prototyping:
- Designed, coordinated, and implemented 20KLOC prototype for major component of MVS.

Negotiation:
- Coordinated design efforts and strategic directions of four IBM divisions for a major VM component.

Testing:
- Wrote, coordinated, and tracked component test plan for MVS Supervisor (OS/VS2 Release 2).

Integration:
- Key technical planner in development of build plan for OS/VS2 Release 2 (MVS).

Installation/ Maintenance:
- Converted three data centers from MVS/SP to MVS/XA.
- Installed and serviced the following major systems and system components

ACHIEVEMENTS CLEARLY CATEGORIZED.

MVS/XA	MVS/SP	VM/370	IMS/VS
TSO/E	VTAM	JES 2	JES 3
RACF	DFP	DF/EF	TCAM
ISPF	NJE	RMF	3270/Session
TSO	UCC7	DMS/OS	Mgr.
APL/SV			

MEANINGFUL DETAILS TO TECHNICAL EMPLOYERS.

and numerous additional program products.

Planning:
- Specified and justified hardware/software systems in support of growth and changing demands of education department for IBM's Data Systems Division.

—continued—

COMBINED

51

Mike Rochip   Page 2

Tuning:	• Supervised performance measurement and tuning of MVS installation containing interactive (IMS, TSO, APL.SV, and IIS) and batch. Accomplished both in a native and VM production guest environment.
	• Led division task force to reduce path length in paging-related components of MVS (OS/VS2 Release 2); impacted five system components, resulted in path-length reduction in excess of 25%.
	• Headed IBM corporate task force to solve MVS V2CR problem.

Instruction:

A SPECIAL CATEGORY OF EXPERIENCE.

• Created and taught courses in Languages, DB/DC, operating systems, teleprocessing, and system diagnostics.
• Designed/developed productivity enhancing software tools:
    • IMS to TSO interface (interactive DL/I).
    • Full-screen editor for IBM 2250 (1981).
    • Interactive system of programs to plan, model, and schedule activities of four teams of instructors.
• Designed and taught seminars on effective use of visual aids (video taped and used as standard training aid for IBM instructors and managers).
• Developed and taught electronics specialty upgrade courses for SAC headquarters electronics technicians.

Technical
Publications:

• "MVS-VM/370 Cohabitation — Making the Marriage Work"
• "Dynamic Generation and Control of Large Data Bases for Interactive Systems Testing"
• "Large System Effects in MVS"
• "Cache Cross-Interrogate Effects in an N-Way MVS System"

THE ICING ON THE CAKE.

Software Patents: • "Dynamic Quickcell Function" — status = file

EMPLOYMENT HISTORY:

A BRIEF CHRONOLOGICAL HISTORY.

1980-Present	Chemical Bank Atlanta, GA	Consultant: System Programmer
1976-1980	IBM Corporation Poughkeepsie, NY	Designer, Team Leader, Systems Programmer/Analyst, Instructor, Field Engineer
1972-1976	U.S. Air Force Offutt AFB Omaha, NE	Digital Electronics Systems Technician, Cryptographer, Instructor

EDUCATION:

Clemson University	BA - Mathematics	1971

Resume Example #4a: A former academic having made the jump into the world of business.

DELL N. HARCOURT

42 Community Circle   Home: (305) 940-4090
Orlando, Florida 32801   Office: (305) 094-9409

EMPLOYMENT
EXPERIENCE

5/81 - Present   Barfield & Ivanovich, Inc.   Senior Editor of
                      Orlando, Florida   Social Studies and History

                      Acquisition and publication of professional/reference text-
                      books.

COST SAVINGS.   ● Cancelled 20 outdated and unwanted contracts without ex-
                        pense or litigation, saving an estimated $500,000.
                      ● Revamped existing list of social studies texts, more than
                        doubling revenue over a 2-year period.
                      ● Established and published a profitable selection of history
                        books, leading to the creation of new Assistant Editor po-
                        sition.

8/77 - 4/81   Hazard House Publishing Company   Social Sciences Editor
                      New York, New York

                      Acquisition and publication of college textbooks.   SPECIFIC
                                                                             ACHIEVEMENTS.

                      ● Redefined short- and medium-range publishing priorities
                        in fields of psychology and sociology.
                      ● Increased profitability of list by 44% during a period of
                        budget reductions.
MANAGERIAL   ● Improved communications between editorial and sales
ACHIEVEMENT.   staff, resulting in largest single year sales increase in
                        11 years.

9/71 - 6/77   New York University   Assistant Professor of Psychology
                      New York, New York

                      ● Conducted graduate and undergraduate classes in   ACADEMIC.
                        behavioral and clinical psychology.
                      ● Initiated liaisons between department and college pub-
                        lishing houses, resulting in 50-60 graduate students
                        serving as management reviewers.

RELATED   Consultant to Hazard House Publishing Company while
PROFESSIONAL   teaching at New York University.
ACTIVITIES
                      Advisor to New York State Behavioral Research Center.

                      Page One

EMPHASIZES
BUSINESS
BACKGROUND;   **CHRONOLOGICAL**
UNDERPLAYS
ACADEMIC
EXPERIENCE.

53

PUBLICATIONS	1982 - ''Behavior in an Industrial Society'' (with Dr. I.H. Feuerbach) - Barfield & Ivanovich.
RELEVANT TO ACADEMIA AND PUBLISHING.	1980 - ''The Inhuman Time Bomb'' (edited readings) - Irving Press.
	1973-1983 - Twenty-two articles and monographs in professional journals (including ''The Behaviorist'') and popular publications (including ''Psychology Tomorrow'').
EDUCATION	1971 - Ph.D., Clinical Psychology, University of California at Los Angeles.
	1968 - M.A., Industrial Psychology, Kent State University, Kent, Ohio.
	1966 - B.A., Psychology, Youngstown State University, Youngstown, Ohio.
FOREIGN LANGUAGES	German. **COULD DELETE.**

Resume Example #4b: Here is the same person as in #4a, but with his background presented functionally.

DELL N. HARCOURT

42 Community Circle   Home (305) 940-4090
Orlando, Florida 32801   Office (305) 094-9409

OBJECTIVE

`TO THE POINT.`

The editorial directorship of a major social sciences and humanities publishing department in higher education.

SUMMARY OF QUALIFICATIONS

Over six years of highly successful editorial acquisitions, including extensive experience in: product development/planning/budgeting/marketing/management/staff supervision and training, with Barfield & Ivanovich (Orlando) and Hazard House (New York).

`EMPHASIZES PUBLISHING BACKGROUND.`

PROFESSIONAL ACHIEVEMENTS

Product Development
● Published highly profitable selection of academic textbooks, increasing revenue by more than 100% (over a 2-year period) and increasing profitability by 44% (during a period of budget cutbacks).

`COMPLETE STATEMENT.`

Planning and Budgeting
● Established editorial priorities for one and five year plans, including budget requirements and projected revenues.
● Saved an estimated $500,000 by cancelling outdated and unwanted contracts without expense or litigation.

`ACCOMPLISHMENTS ARE PLACED IN A MEANINGFUL CONTEXT.`

Marketing
● Produced accurate and meaningful data for marketing and sales staff, contributing to exceptionally high sales increase.

Management, Supervision and Training
● Coordinated work-flow of copy and production editors, publishing schedules, and daily interaction with more than 25 authors.
● Supervised two junior acquisitions editors, both of whom were subsequently promoted.
● Implemented visible and successful on-the-job training program for editorial assistants.

RELATED PROFESSIONAL ACTIVITIES

Assistant Professor of Psychology, New York University.

Consultant to Hazard House (while teaching).

`DOWNPLAYS ACADEMIC BACKGROUND.`

Advisor to New York State Behavioral Research Center.

`AN ALTERNATIVE TO #4A; PERHAPS MORE EFFECTIVE.`

FUNCTIONAL

55

PUBLICATIONS

    1982: "Behavior in an Industrial Society" (with Dr. I.H. Feuerbach) - Barfield & Ivanovich.

    1980: "The Inhuman Time Bomb" (edited readings) - Irving Press.

    1979-1983: Twenty-two articles and monographs in professional and popular journals.

EDUCATION

    1971: Ph.D., Clinical Psychology, University of California at Los Angeles.

    1968: M.A., Industrial Psychology, Kent State University, Ohio.

    1966: B.A., Psychology, Youngstown State University, Ohio.

FOREIGN LANGUAGES
    German.

Resume Example #5: Leaving the military; seeking a career in business.

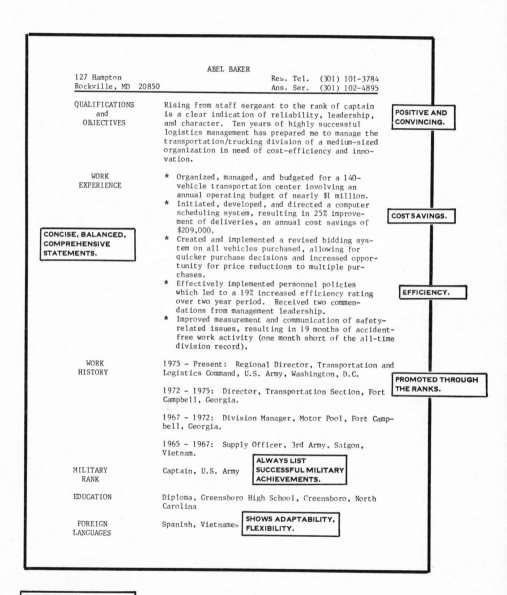

ABEL BAKER

127 Hampton
Rockville, MD 20850

Res. Tel. (301) 101-3784
Ans. Ser. (301) 102-4895

QUALIFICATIONS and OBJECTIVES

Rising from staff sergeant to the rank of captain is a clear indication of reliability, leadership, and character. Ten years of highly successful logistics management has prepared me to manage the transportation/trucking division of a medium-sized organization in need of cost-efficiency and innovation.

POSITIVE AND CONVINCING.

WORK EXPERIENCE

* Organized, managed, and budgeted for a 140-vehicle transportation center involving an annual operating budget of nearly $1 million.
* Initiated, developed, and directed a computer scheduling system, resulting in 25% improvement of deliveries, an annual cost savings of $209,000.

COST SAVINGS.

CONCISE, BALANCED, COMPREHENSIVE STATEMENTS.

* Created and implemented a revised bidding system on all vehicles purchased, allowing for quicker purchase decisions and increased opportunity for price reductions to multiple purchases.
* Effectively implemented personnel policies which led to a 19% increased efficiency rating over two year period. Received two commendations from management leadership.

EFFICIENCY.

* Improved measurement and communication of safety-related issues, resulting in 19 months of accident-free work activity (one month short of the all-time division record).

WORK HISTORY

1975 - Present: Regional Director, Transportation and Logistics Command, U.S. Army, Washington, D.C.

PROMOTED THROUGH THE RANKS.

1972 - 1975: Director, Transportation Section, Fort Campbell, Georgia.

1967 - 1972: Division Manager, Motor Pool, Fort Campbell, Georgia.

1965 - 1967: Supply Officer, 3rd Army, Saigon, Vietnam.

MILITARY RANK

Captain, U.S. Army

ALWAYS LIST SUCCESSFUL MILITARY ACHIEVEMENTS.

EDUCATION

Diploma, Greensboro High School, Greensboro, North Carolina

FOREIGN LANGUAGES

Spanish, Vietnamese

SHOWS ADAPTABILITY, FLEXIBILITY.

EMPHASIZING SKILLS AND EXPERIENCE THAT ARE OF INTEREST TO POTENTIAL EMPLOYERS: DEEMPHASIZING THOSE THAT ARE LESS RELEVANT.

COMBINED

Resume Example #6: A hospital care specialist demonstrates his versatility and broad range of skills.

SHERMAN N. PEABODY

1 Maywood Road
Roanoke, VA 24014

Residence: (804) 001-0001
Business: (804) 100-1000

EDUCATION:

M.B.A. — Howard University, 1978.
M.A. — Jackson State, 1976. Guidance and Counseling.
B.S. — Morgan State, 1969. Economics and Business Administration.

EXPERIENCE:
October 1984
to Present

MEDICAL CARE ASSOCIATES, Asheville, NC
GENERAL MANAGER

Directly responsible for all operations of a Medicare certified home health agency with annual revenue of $4,200,000. Major services include: Home health care, private duty care and supplemental staffing. 900 full and part-time employees; 5 branch offices.
- *Reorganized* internal operations resulting in monthly savings of $10,000.
- *Implemented* marketing programs and internal controls that resulted in 20% increase in sales.
- *Managed* successful transition from franchise operation to corporate branch.
- *Directed* implementation of computerized client and employee information system.

> **DEMONSTRATES ORIENTATION AND VALUE OF MANAGEMENT ACTION.**

March 1974 to
October 1984

WALTER A. CUMMINS HOSPITAL SYSTEM, Mobile, AL
DIRECTOR OF MANAGEMENT SERVICES,
BEAUMONT SHARED SERVICES, INC.
(October 1983 to October 1984)
Responsible for several major components of $30,000,000 per year for profit subsidiary of hospital. Responsibilities included: contract management, management consulting, strategic planning, business development, home health care.
- *Planned and implemented* establishment of durable medical equipment subsidiary: generated over $400,000 in revenue, $40,000 in profit during first year.
- *Initiated* first comprehensive strategic planning process for Cummins Shared Services.
- *Expanded* contract management to include four hospitals and various consulting projects: generated revenue in excess of $200,000 per year.
- *Designed* comprehensive wage and benefit program for Shared Services employees, reduced personnel expenses by 15%, but maintained current staffing levels.
- *Invited* to speak as guest lecturer for Alabama Hospital Association on hospitals and home health care.

> **HAS AN EYE FOR EARNINGS.**

ASSISTANT DIRECTOR
(September 1982 to October 1983)
Complete administrative responsibility for patient support departments of 950-bed teaching hospital. Responsible for 520 employees and annual budget of $6,600,000.
- *Planned* and helped initiate conversion of former school into comprehensive outpatient health care center.
- *Organized and conducted* major consulting projects in Nigeria and Saudi Arabia.
- *Initiated* the planning process required to streamline functions of patient service departments.

> **VERSATILE AND ADVENTURESOME.**

CHRONOLOGICAL

> **LAYS IT ALL OUT CLEARLY AND WITH DETAIL.**

Resume Example #6; page two

ARKANSAS COMMUNITY HOSPITAL, Little Rock, AR
ADMINISTRATOR
(September 1980 to August 1982)

Full responsibility for 25-bed acute care hospital with annual budget of $2,500,000.
* *Developed and implemented* comprehensive business plan and budget system.
* *Successfully* recruited two family practitioners to hospital's service area.
* *Successfully* negotiated vendor contracts which reduced expenses by 10%.

NORTH VIRGINIA HOSPITAL SYSTEM, Arlington, VA
ADMINISTRATIVE ASSOCIATE
(February 1978 to August 1980)

Responsible for management functions of Clinical Pathology Department which employed 250. Areas of responsibility included: fiscal management, laboratory and employee representation to administration, operational policies and procedures.

PERSONNEL ASSISTANT
(November 1976 to January 1978)

Responsible for provision of personnel services to all areas of hospital. Developed department's data processing systems. Administered wage and salary and grievance programs.

FINANCIAL ANALYST
(March 1974 to October 1976)

Assisted in preparation of revenue, expense and capital budgets. Prepared and analyzed monthly variance reports and financial statements. Managed hospital's investment portfolio.

February 1971 to March 1974

WOODWORTH DEPARTMENT STORE, Washington, DC
FINANCIAL ANALYST

Two year active duty military obligation fulfilled during this period.

MILITARY SERVICE:

U.S. ARMY
SERGEANT
(March 1971 to March 1973)
Stationed at Pentagon. Honorable discharge.

PERSONAL:

Married, two children.

AFFILIATIONS:

American College of Hospital Administrators (member).

59

Resume Example #7: An ex-offender who has changed his ways makes even the worst of his experiences work for him.

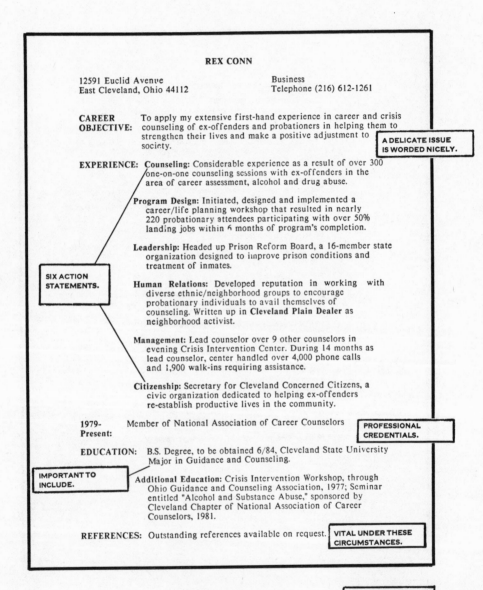

REX CONN

12591 Euclid Avenue
East Cleveland, Ohio 44112

Business
Telephone (216) 612-1261

CAREER OBJECTIVE: To apply my extensive first-hand experience in career and crisis counseling of ex-offenders and probationers in helping them to strengthen their lives and make a positive adjustment to society.

> A DELICATE ISSUE IS WORDED NICELY.

EXPERIENCE: **Counseling:** Considerable experience as a result of over 300 one-on-one counseling sessions with ex-offenders in the area of career assessment, alcohol and drug abuse.

Program Design: Initiated, designed and implemented a career/life planning workshop that resulted in nearly 220 probationary attendees participating with over 50% landing jobs within 6 months of program's completion.

Leadership: Headed up Prison Reform Board, a 16-member state organization designed to improve prison conditions and treatment of inmates.

> SIX ACTION STATEMENTS.

Human Relations: Developed reputation in working with diverse ethnic/neighborhood groups to encourage probationary individuals to avail themselves of counseling. Written up in **Cleveland Plain Dealer** as neighborhood activist.

Management: Lead counselor over 9 other counselors in evening Crisis Intervention Center. During 14 months as lead counselor, center handled over 4,000 phone calls and 1,900 walk-ins requiring assistance.

Citizenship: Secretary for Cleveland Concerned Citizens, a civic organization dedicated to helping ex-offenders re-establish productive lives in the community.

1979-Present: Member of National Association of Career Counselors

> PROFESSIONAL CREDENTIALS.

EDUCATION: B.S. Degree, to be obtained 6/84, Cleveland State University Major in Guidance and Counseling.

> IMPORTANT TO INCLUDE.

Additional Education: Crisis Intervention Workshop, through Ohio Guidance and Counseling Association, 1977; Seminar entitled "Alcohol and Substance Abuse," sponsored by Cleveland Chapter of National Association of Career Counselors, 1981.

REFERENCES: Outstanding references available on request.

> VITAL UNDER THESE CIRCUMSTANCES.

FUNCTIONAL

> TRANSFORMING AN UNFORTUNATE EXPERIENCE INTO A POSITIVE AND OPTIMISTIC CAREER.

Resume Example #8: An administrator planning a career change.

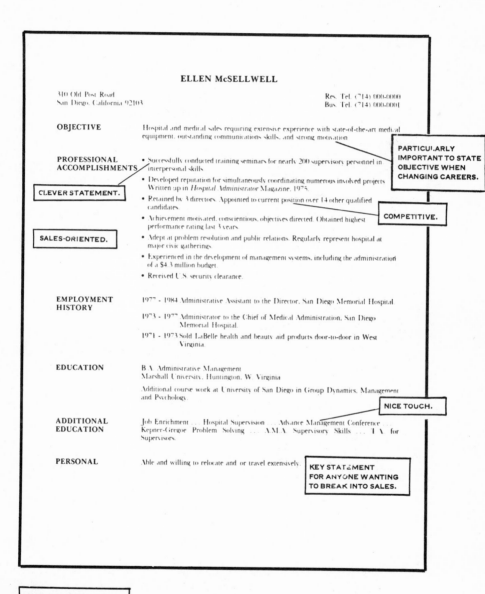

ELLEN McSELLWELL

310 Old Post Road
San Diego, California 92103

Res. Tel. (714) 000-0000
Bus. Tel. (714) 000-0001

OBJECTIVE

Hospital and medical sales requiring extensive experience with state-of-the-art medical equipment, outstanding communications skills, and strong motivation.

> PARTICULARLY IMPORTANT TO STATE OBJECTIVE WHEN CHANGING CAREERS.

PROFESSIONAL ACCOMPLISHMENTS

> CLEVER STATEMENT.

> SALES-ORIENTED.

- Successfully conducted training seminars for nearly 200 supervisory personnel in interpersonal skills.
- Developed reputation for simultaneously coordinating numerous involved projects. Written up in *Hospital Administrator* Magazine, 1975.
- Retained by 3 directors. Appointed to current position over 14 other qualified candidates.

> COMPETITIVE.

- Achievement motivated, conscientious, objectives directed. Obtained highest performance rating last 3 years.
- Adept at problem resolution and public relations. Regularly represent hospital at major civic gatherings.
- Experienced in the development of management systems, including the administration of a $4.3 million budget.
- Received U.S. security clearance.

EMPLOYMENT HISTORY

1977 - 1984 Administrative Assistant to the Director, San Diego Memorial Hospital.

1973 - 1977 Administrator to the Chief of Medical Administration, San Diego Memorial Hospital.

1971 - 1973 Sold LaBelle health and beauty aid products door-to-door in West Virginia.

EDUCATION

B.A. Administrative Management
Marshall University, Huntington, W. Virginia

Additional course work at University of San Diego in Group Dynamics, Management and Psychology.

> NICE TOUCH.

ADDITIONAL EDUCATION

Job Enrichment .... Hospital Supervision .... Advance Management Conference .... Kepner-Gregoe Problem Solving .... A.M.A. Supervisory Skills .... T.A. for Supervisors.

PERSONAL

Able and willing to relocate and/or travel extensively.

> KEY STATEMENT FOR ANYONE WANTING TO BREAK INTO SALES.

> UTILIZING SKILLS AND ACCOMPLISHMENTS TO CONSTRUCT A NEW CAREER.

COMBINED

Resume Example #9: A research scientist who _isn't_ looking for a job, at present.

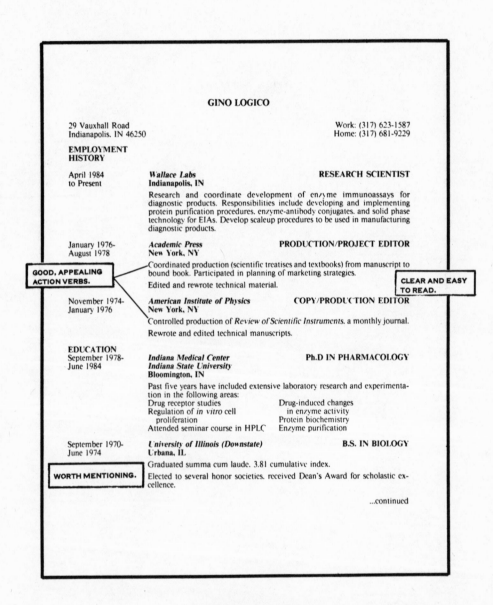

GINO LOGICO

29 Vauxhall Road
Indianapolis. IN 46250

Work: (317) 623-1587
Home: (317) 681-9229

EMPLOYMENT HISTORY

April 1984 to Present

Wallace Labs
Indianapolis, IN

RESEARCH SCIENTIST

Research and coordinate development of enzyme immunoassays for diagnostic products. Responsibilities include developing and implementing protein purification procedures. enzyme-antibody conjugates. and solid phase technology for EIAs. Develop scaleup procedures to be used in manufacturing diagnostic products.

January 1976-
August 1978

Academic Press
New York, NY

PRODUCTION/PROJECT EDITOR

Coordinated production (scientific treatises and textbooks) from manuscript to bound book. Participated in planning of marketing strategies.

Edited and rewrote technical material.

GOOD, APPEALING ACTION VERBS.

CLEAR AND EASY TO READ.

November 1974-
January 1976

American Institute of Physics
New York, NY

COPY/PRODUCTION EDITOR

Controlled production of _Review of Scientific Instruments_. a monthly journal.

Rewrote and edited technical manuscripts.

EDUCATION
September 1978-
June 1984

Indiana Medical Center
Indiana State University
Bloomington, IN

Ph.D IN PHARMACOLOGY

Past five years have included extensive laboratory research and experimentation in the following areas:
Drug receptor studies
Regulation of _in vitro_ cell
   proliferation
Attended seminar course in HPLC

Drug-induced changes
  in enzyme activity
Protein biochemistry
Enzyme purification

September 1970-
June 1974

University of Illinois (Downstate)
Urbana, IL

B.S. IN BIOLOGY

Graduated summa cum laude. 3.81 cumulative index.

WORTH MENTIONING.

Elected to several honor societies. received Dean's Award for scholastic excellence.

...continued

CHRONOLOGICAL

Resume Example #9; page two

GINO LOGICO

page 2

| PUBLICATIONS | March 1985: *Biochemical Pharmocology* (Vol. 34. No. 6. pp. 811-819). Title. Effect of streptozotocin on the glutathione S-transferases of mouse liver cytosol. |

IMPORTANT FOR A RESEARCHER.

August 1982: *Journal of Laboratory and Clinical Medicine* (Vol. 100. No. 2. pp. 178-185). Title: Identification of a glucocorticoid receptor in the human leukemia cell line K562.

November 1981: *Blood* (Vol. 58. NO. 5. Suppl. 1. p. 120a). Abstract-same title as article above.

RELATED ACTIVITIES

Downstate: Instruction of medical students in pharmacology.
U. of IN: Tutored undergraduate students in science and mathematics.

SPECIAL SKILLS

Personal computers. including word processing.

NICE ADDITION.

PERSONAL DATA

Married. two children.

UNNECESSARY, BUT CAN'T HURT.

63

Example #10: A graduating senior with very little experience searches for his first job.

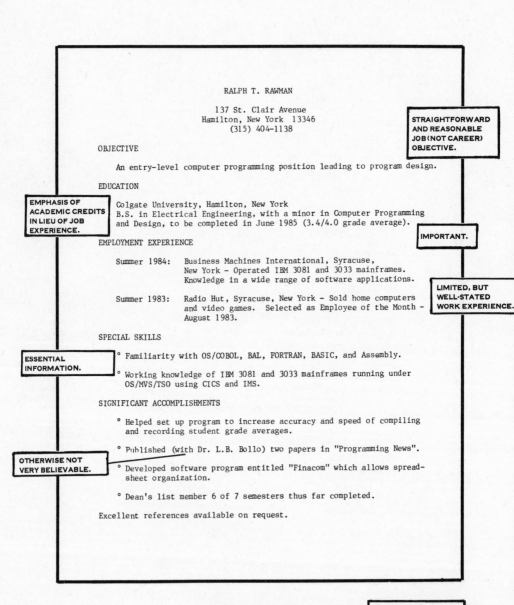

RALPH T. RAWMAN

137 St. Clair Avenue
Hamilton, New York 13346
(315) 404-1138

STRAIGHTFORWARD
AND REASONABLE
JOB (NOT CAREER)
OBJECTIVE.

OBJECTIVE

An entry-level computer programming position leading to program design.

EDUCATION

EMPHASIS OF
ACADEMIC CREDITS
IN LIEU OF JOB
EXPERIENCE.

Colgate University, Hamilton, New York
B.S. in Electrical Engineering, with a minor in Computer Programming
and Design, to be completed in June 1985 (3.4/4.0 grade average).

IMPORTANT.

EMPLOYMENT EXPERIENCE

Summer 1984: Business Machines International, Syracuse,
New York - Operated IBM 3081 and 3033 mainframes.
Knowledge in a wide range of software applications.

Summer 1983: Radio Hut, Syracuse, New York - Sold home computers
and video games. Selected as Employee of the Month -
August 1983.

LIMITED, BUT
WELL-STATED
WORK EXPERIENCE.

SPECIAL SKILLS

ESSENTIAL
INFORMATION.

° Familiarity with OS/COBOL, BAL, FORTRAN, BASIC, and Assembly.

° Working knowledge of IBM 3081 and 3033 mainframes running under
OS/MVS/TSO using CICS and IMS.

SIGNIFICANT ACCOMPLISHMENTS

° Helped set up program to increase accuracy and speed of compiling
and recording student grade averages.

° Published (with Dr. L.B. Bollo) two papers in "Programming News".

OTHERWISE NOT
VERY BELIEVABLE.

° Developed software program entitled "Finacom" which allows spread-
sheet organization.

° Dean's list member 6 of 7 semesters thus far completed.

Excellent references available on request.

FUNCTIONAL

MAKES THE MOST
OUT OF VERY LITTLE.

Resume Example #11: A middle-aged executive looking for a top-management spot.

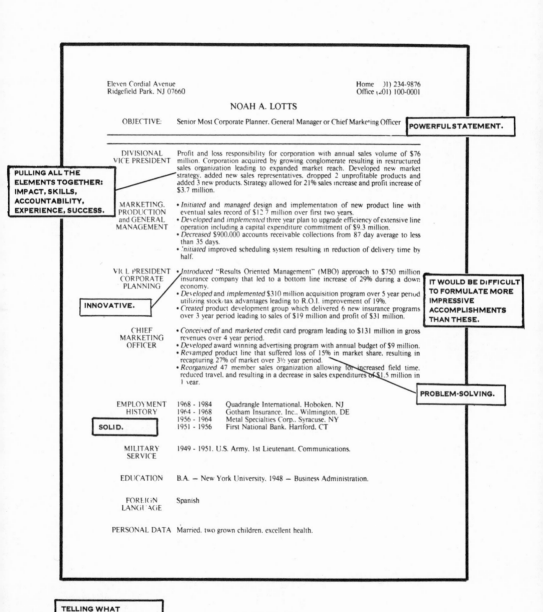

Eleven Cordial Avenue
Ridgefield Park. NJ 07660

Home)1) 234-9876
Office (201) 100-0001

NOAH A. LOTTS

OBJECTIVE: Senior Most Corporate Planner. General Manager or Chief Marketing Officer

> **POWERFUL STATEMENT.**

DIVISIONAL VICE PRESIDENT
Profit and loss responsibility for corporation with annual sales volume of $76 million. Corporation acquired by growing conglomerate resulting in restructured sales organization leading to expanded market reach. Developed new market strategy. added new sales representatives. dropped 2 unprofitable products and added 3 new products. Strategy allowed for 21% sales increase and profit increase of $3.7 million.

> **PULLING ALL THE ELEMENTS TOGETHER: IMPACT, SKILLS, ACCOUNTABILITY, EXPERIENCE, SUCCESS.**

MARKETING. PRODUCTION and GENERAL MANAGEMENT
- *Initiated* and *managed* design and implementation of new product line with eventual sales record of $12.7 million over first two years.
- *Developed* and *implemented* three year plan to upgrade efficiency of extensive line operation including a capital expenditure commitment of $9.3 million.
- *Decreased* $900.000 accounts receivable collections from 87 day average to less than 35 days.
- *Initiated* improved scheduling system resulting in reduction of delivery time by half.

VICE PRESIDENT CORPORATE PLANNING
- *Introduced* "Results Oriented Management" (MBO) approach to $750 million insurance company that led to a bottom line increase of 29% during a down economy.
- *Developed* and *implemented* $310 million acquisition program over 5 year period utilizing stock/tax advantages leading to R.O.I. improvement of 19%.
- *Created* product development group which delivered 6 new insurance programs over 3 year period leading to sales of $19 million and profit of $31 million.

> **INNOVATIVE.**

> **IT WOULD BE DIFFICULT TO FORMULATE MORE IMPRESSIVE ACCOMPLISHMENTS THAN THESE.**

CHIEF MARKETING OFFICER
- *Conceived* of and *marketed* credit card program leading to $131 million in gross revenues over 4 year period.
- *Developed* award winning advertising program with annual budget of $9 million.
- *Revamped* product line that suffered loss of 15% in market share. resulting in recapturing 27% of market over 3½ year period.
- *Reorganized* 47 member sales organization allowing for increased field time. reduced travel. and resulting in a decrease in sales expenditures of $1.5 million in 1 year.

> **PROBLEM-SOLVING.**

EMPLOYMENT HISTORY
1968 - 1984	Quadrangle International. Hoboken. NJ
1964 - 1968	Gotham Insurance. Inc.. Wilmington. DE
1956 - 1964	Metal Specialties Corp.. Syracuse. NY
1951 - 1956	First National Bank. Hartford. CT

> **SOLID.**

MILITARY SERVICE
1949 - 1951. U.S. Army. 1st Lieutenant. Communications.

EDUCATION
B.A. — New York University. 1948 — Business Administration.

FOREIGN LANGUAGE
Spanish

PERSONAL DATA
Married. two grown children. excellent health.

> **TELLING WHAT YOU'VE DONE WITH DIGNITY WHEN THERE IS A GOOD DEAL TO TALK ABOUT.**

COMBINED

Resume Example #12: An engineer with well-chosen accomplishment statements and a marketing flair.

JULIO IGLESIAS GARCIA

1001 Asuncion   Tel: 800-123-4567
San Juan, PR 00920

EMPLOYMENT   Carib Electro Corporation, San Juan--Service and Quality Control Manager.
1977   Responsible for field and customer service activities along with quality
TO   control inspection of equipment to insure compliance with customer, OSHA
PRESENT   and JIC standards. Additional responsibilities include purchasing and
              technical service manual writing.

              * Organized 6-person service department to perform SAE certification
                testing verification of systems, resulting in 60% increase in contract

ATTENTION:
PROSPECTIVE   revenues along with warranty and non-warranty repairs, which led to an
EMPLOYERS.   increase in repeat sales of 45%.

              * Wrote technical operation and maintenance manuals for all systems
                manufactured.

              * Reduced purchasing costs 32% by developing and utilizing purchasing
                program for TRS80 computer.   **BOTTOM-LINE**
                                                                        ORIENTED.
              * Developed quality control procedures resulting in 60% decrease in
                warranty service calls.

1973   ABZ Corporation, Xeroradiography Division--Technical Specialist. Responsible
TO   for field service and support of all technical representatives and con-
1977   tractors within designated region.

              * Promoted from technical representative in Ponce branch to specialist
                within 9 months of employment and became responsible for San Juan
                territory.

              * Reduced nationwide service call rate by developing and implementing
                various in-field system retrofits.

              * Relocated to develop new area in Denver (CO)-based territory which
                resulted in area sales increase of 35 systems the following year.   **GETS RESULTS.**

EDUCATION   New York University, November 1983--Bachelor of Applied Science, Electronic
              Engineering Technology. Graduated with 3.95/4.0 G.P.A.; primary con-
              centrations in business communication, personnel administration, human
DRAWS OUT BUSINESS   resource management, business law, principles of marketing and behavioral
AND HUMAN BEHAVIOR   psychology.
CLASSES.

              RETS Electronic, June 1973--Associates Degree in Electronic Engineering
              Technology. Second Class FCC Radio Telephone license.

ACTIVITIES   Participating member of Society of Technical Communication (STC).

SPECIAL   Bilingual, English/Spanish.
SKILLS
                                          ESSENTIAL FOR
                                          THIS LOCATION.

CHRONOLOGICAL

Resume Example #13: A mid-level manager looking to make a substantial jump in responsibility.

ERIC VON HOHAUSER

79 Brampton Street
Bismarck, ND 58010

Res. 701/110-1001
Bus. 701/001-0110

PROFESSIONAL EXPERIENCE: Twelve years of administrative and sales management in finance and insurance.

As Financial Services Manager for Life Enhancement Insurance Co., responsible on a national basis for new account installations, new business development, and marketing of financial products. Conduct seminar presentations to potential customer groups on a variety of financial topics relating to our product capabilities. Extremely knowledgeable concerning all phases of consumer lending regulations. Headed up project and marketed microcomputer system that has now been installed in over 300 credit unions. Designed and implemented an IRA product which has been sold to over 100 credit unions in first six months.

While at Laurel Schools Credit Union, was Operations Officer directly responsible for internal operations of this $22 million financial institution with 33 employees. Was Chief Operating Officer, personally administered all lending activities, accounting, staff training, loan delinquencies, and work flow scheduling. Implemented revolving credit loan system. Designed marketing promotions and more efficient services resulting in assets increasing from $10 million to $22 million in two years.

While at Manufacturers Mortgage, originated and handled underwriting for short-term commercial construction loans, supervised $20 million portfolio. At Monroe Bank & Trust, designed operating procedures for branch office and main office departments. developed procedures for implementation of Master Charge system, conducted training sessions with over 300 branch personnel. Conducted analysis resulting in purchase and installation of such equipment as high-speed check photographing machines, branch camera equipment, and teller machines.

POSITIONS:

5/77 - Present:	Life Enhancement Ins. Co.	Manager, Financial Services
4/75 - 5/77:	Laurel Schools Credit Union	Operations Officer
10/72 - 4/75:	Manufacturers Mortgage	Commercial Loan Officer
1/68- 10/72:	Monroe Bank & Trust	Operations Analyst

COMMUNITY ACTIVITIES:
Chairman, Administration Committee for St. Michael's Parish.

Member, Citizens Advisory Group for Board of Education.

EDUCATION:
B.B.A. 1968, University of Miami, Business Administration.

HIGHLIGHTS SALES AND PRODUCT MANAGEMENT CAPABILITIES.

POINTS OUT GENERAL MANAGEMENT EXPERIENCE.

GOOD FINAL PARAGRAPH THAT COVERS A VARIETY OF ADMINISTRATIVE TALENTS.

EACH OF THE 3 PARAGRAPHS ILLUSTRATES A SET OF SKILLS WHICH SHOWS THIS INDIVIDUAL'S VERSATILITY.

FUNCTIONAL

Resume Example #14: A highly-experienced, versatile professional manager who puts his best foot forward.

CHRISTOPHER LIBIDOS

42 East 73rd Avenue
Tulsa, OK 74115

Home: 405/000-0000
Office: 405/000-0000

ABILITY TO IDENTIFY, FORMULATE, AND MARKET HIGH PAYOFF PROJECTS:
Developed projects that led to birth of 6,000 terminal communications network, $20 million-a-year wholesale company (the Arbor House Specials seen on TV), installing M.B.O., annual marketing plan in division of 1450, and an accounting system for bookstores.

ABILITY TO START, GROW AND MANAGE DEPARTMENTS: Started and managed: 5 training departments, research department, personnel department, and district sales office. Played key role starting 70 national account sales departments and 2 research departments.

P&L RESPONSIBILITY: Started division with $66,500 budget; now over $2.8 million.

ABILITY TO WORK AT TOP LEVELS: Setting up board summit meetings to develop corporate objectives. Directly responsible to board for several projects. Staff person in charge of several board committees. Sold and serviced group coverage working with top management and unions of major companies. Three years as Management Consultant.

SCOPE OF TRAINING EXPERIENCE: Managing and doing: Sales training, management and organization development, plus clerical and technical training. Developing, staffing, and selling 50 workshops with 5,000 enrollees per year, throughout North America, regarding: financial and marketing management. Producer of workbooks, movies, programmed instruction and video programs.

SCOPE OF RESEARCH EXPERIENCE: Managing: Market research, new product development, operations improvement, R&D, and fact base development and maintenance. Create and conduct census of retail flower shops; primary source of data for floral industry.

POSITIONS:

1976 - Present	Director, Education and Research Division Arbor House. International association; 1200 retail bookstores.
1973 - 1976	Management Consultant for consulting firm of Martell and Coxwell, Inc. Worked with National Association of Blue Cross Plans, Midas Muffler, and Continental Airlines.
1961 - 1963	Manager Employee Development Dept., Ohio Blue Cross.
1955 - 1961	Manager of various sales, training and personnel functions, including the Automobile Club of Ohio.

EDUCATION: B.A. Economics, Washington State University, Seattle, Washington.
Over 1500 classroom hours at: University of Tulsa, University of Chicago, Ohio State University.
Re: Management, Mathematics, Organization Development, Behavioral Sciences, and Educational Technology.

WELL-PHRASED HEADINGS.

COMBINATION OF EXPERIENCES SHOWS BOTH VERSATILITY AND DEPTH.

EMPHASIS HERE IS ON CONTINUING EDUCATION.

COMBINED

HERE'S ADDITIONAL PROOF THAT A ONE-PAGE RESUME CAN PROVIDE IMPACT.

Resume Example #15: *A high-level executive who gets it all onto a single page.*

ROGER M.B. ARMAND

14 McCaul Street
Toronto, Ontario MST IWI

home (416) 562-1514
office (416) 917-8285

Professional
Experience

1983-
Present

PUBLICATION SERVICES ASSOCIATES, INC., Toronto, Ontario

President & Principal — Promote and furnish cost-efficient microcomputer systems to publishing companies. Assist in selection of appropriate hardware and softwares designed to save time, control costs, increase editorial and marketing productivity.

> HE SAYS A LOT
> WITH A FEW
> WELL-CHOSEN WORDS.

1973-
1982

THOMPSON PUBLICATIONS, Toronto, Ontario

President & CEO — Chief executive in charge of operations for a leading vocational/technical textbook publisher. Exercise P&L authority for all phases of management, including editorial, production, and marketing, with 70 employees reporting.

Executive Vice-President — Reporting to the Chairman of the Board.
Administered daily operations of Delmar Publishers in Albany, NY. Position combined general management authority with supervision of marketing and sales staff. Established computerized sales information system, resulting in better allocation of sales territories and improvements in capital investment in publishing projects.

> WHEN YOU HAVE
> ACCOMPLISHED THIS
> MUCH, DETAILS CAN BE
> SAFELY SUMMARIZED.

Director, Marketing & Sales — Directed all marketing activities, including advertising, direct mail promotion, product releases, exhibits, and field selling. Developed computer data base of mailing lists, and organized sales communication system for timely reportage by field sales representatives.

1966-
1973

McGRAW-HILL BOOK COMPANY OF CANADA, Toronto, Ontario

Held key positions in Marketing & Sales Administration with three textbook divisions: Gregg, Community College, and Technical/Vocational. Achievements include development of first integrated product information system for college and technical/vocational titles; introduced Professional Selling Skills program to college travelers; designed and published *Technical Education News* quarterly magazine; instrumental in converting catalogs to computer data base for electronic typesetting.

Education

1975 — MBA, University of Toronto Graduate School of Business Administration.

1965 — BA, McGill University, Montreal.

CHRONOLOGICAL

Resume Example #16: Deemphasizing unemployment by focusing on experience, accomplishments, and educational background.

EDWARD SHANGE-YEE
1404 Second Avenue, West Haven CT 06516   203/302-3020

EYE-CATCHING FORMAT.

OBJECTIVE
To utilize my fiscal skills and administrative abilities to do research, analyze and develop fiscal policies within a leading corporation.

QUALIFIED BY
Seven years of experience including:

EXCELLENT SUMMARY TELLS US WHAT TO LOOK FOR.

- Major Fiscal Responsibilities
- Policy Development for the State of Massachusetts
- Applied Research
- Training in Public Accounting and Finance

- Staff Training
- Leadership and Planning
- Extensive Training in Statistics
- Training in Benefits and Compensation Management

SPECIFIC ACCOMPLISHMENTS CANNOT BE EXPECTED FROM A YOUNGER PERSON.

CLEVERLY ARRANGED AND UTILIZED SPACE.

EDUCATION
M.B.A. IN MANAGEMENT, University Massachusetts, Amherst, MA, 1983
-Major areas of concentration:
  Management and Accounting

EXCEPTIONALLY IMPRESSIVE EDUCATION MAY BE PLACED AHEAD OF JOB EXPERIENCE.

B.S. IN PSYCHOLOGY, Amherst University, Amherst, MA, 1979
-Major areas of concentration:
  Psychology and Statistics
-Graduated Cum Laude

Currently preparing for C.P.A. Exam
-Major area of concentration: Taxation
-Completing final coursework in Accounting

ACHIEVEMENTS
Fiscal Analysis
Identified excess capacity at the state laboratory allowing for an internally-funded expansion to out-of-state sales, resulting in increased revenues of over $2 million. Developed tax planning, record keeping and income tax service for small businesses and individuals.

BOTTOM-LINE IMPACT.

FUNCTIONAL

THE KIND OF RESUME POTENTIAL EMPLOYERS LIKE TO READ: NEAT, CLEARLY-ORGANIZED, OBJECTIVE.

EDWARD SHANGE-YEE

Organization/Administration
Organized and supervised the personnel department for a nonprofit organization serving over 300 members.

Leadership/Planning
Supervised the development of a computerized budget tracking system for the state budget process.

Research
Evaluated effectiveness of state programs, resulting in increased efficiency and program planning. Supervised market research students in evaluating the impact and utilization of promotional media.

EXPERIENCE
Financial Manager
Responsible for $2 million of the Department of Public Health budget including policy development, evaluation of program effectiveness, review of budget requests, and participation in special task forces.

Massachusetts Department of Public Health, 1981 to 1983.

> **VERY IMPRESSIVE BACKGROUND FOR A RECENT GRAD.**

Social Research Analyst
Conduct policy analyses, program evaluation and subsequent statistical analysis.

Massachusetts Department of Management and Budget, 1979 to 1980.

Management Consultant
Conducted market research, fiscal analyses, tax and economic planning for nonprofit organizations, individuals, and small businesses.

Assistant Manager
Responsible for personnel supervision, ordering, cash reports, budgeting

PROFESSIONAL MEMBERSHIPS
- American Management Association
- Association of M.B.A. Executives

> **RELEVANT MEMBERSHIPS.**

PERSONAL
Married, 1 child.

> **UNNECESSARY BUT OK.**

Resume Example #17: *An unemployed professional looking for a new job.*

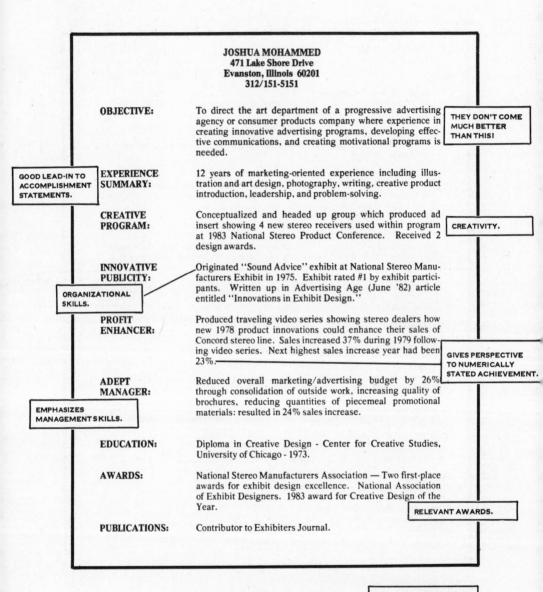

JOSHUA MOHAMMED
471 Lake Shore Drive
Evanston, Illinois 60201
312/151-5151

OBJECTIVE: To direct the art department of a progressive advertising agency or consumer products company where experience in creating innovative advertising programs, developing effective communications, and creating motivational programs is needed.

THEY DON'T COME MUCH BETTER THAN THIS!

EXPERIENCE SUMMARY: 12 years of marketing-oriented experience including illustration and art design, photography, writing, creative product introduction, leadership, and problem-solving.

GOOD LEAD-IN TO ACCOMPLISHMENT STATEMENTS.

CREATIVE PROGRAM: Conceptualized and headed up group which produced ad insert showing 4 new stereo receivers used within program at 1983 National Stereo Product Conference. Received 2 design awards.

CREATIVITY.

INNOVATIVE PUBLICITY: Originated "Sound Advice" exhibit at National Stereo Manufacturers Exhibit in 1975. Exhibit rated #1 by exhibit participants. Written up in Advertising Age (June '82) article entitled "Innovations in Exhibit Design."

ORGANIZATIONAL SKILLS.

PROFIT ENHANCER: Produced traveling video series showing stereo dealers how new 1978 product innovations could enhance their sales of Concord stereo line. Sales increased 37% during 1979 following video series. Next highest sales increase year had been 23%.

GIVES PERSPECTIVE TO NUMERICALLY STATED ACHIEVEMENT.

ADEPT MANAGER: Reduced overall marketing/advertising budget by 26% through consolidation of outside work, increasing quality of brochures, reducing quantities of piecemeal promotional materials: resulted in 24% sales increase.

EMPHASIZES MANAGEMENT SKILLS.

EDUCATION: Diploma in Creative Design - Center for Creative Studies, University of Chicago - 1973.

AWARDS: National Stereo Manufacturers Association — Two first-place awards for exhibit design excellence. National Association of Exhibit Designers. 1983 award for Creative Design of the Year.

RELEVANT AWARDS.

PUBLICATIONS: Contributor to Exhibiters Journal.

FUNCTIONAL

DRAWS ATTENTION AWAY FROM QUESTION OF UNEMPLOYMENT IN A POSITIVE MANNER.

72

Resume Example #18: A recent college graduate who makes an excellent representation of her brief but relevant work experience.

ADELAIDE B. APPLEBY
147 Deerwood Lane
Cedar Rapids, IA 52404
(309) 000-0001

OBJECTIVE
A position in financial administration, financial analysis, financial planning, or funds management in a progressive organization that will require my best efforts.

EDUCATION
B.A. Financial Administration, June 1985
Iowa State University
GPA: 3.5/4.0

PROFESSIONAL EMPLOYMENT
Summers 1983 & 1984: Holt Corp., Alpha Insulation Division, Iowa City.

● *Financial Analyst:* Analyzed operating, pricing, and purchasing variances weekly. Prepared financial performance reports. Provided financial analysis for special projects. Took part in year-end closing and LIFO cost calculations. Attended budget and forecasting meetings with senior management. Interacted in various controllership duties.

● *Inventory Control:* Planned and conducted verification systems for the Direct Salesforce to accurately report status of inventories. Audited and reconciled inventories of the vans, mini-warehouses and regional warehouses. Recommended methods to reduce inventory shrinkage.

● *Credit Analyst:* Responsible for USA Direct Sell operations. Approved or rejected sales orders from customers. Reviewed and revised customer credit limits. Wrote 80-page procedure manual for the Credit Department to help establish a consistent credit policy. Negotiated special rates with the collection agencies.

POSITIONS HELD WHILE ATTENDING COLLEGE
1981-1985 Part-time: Iowa State University
Student Assistant: Duties included processing journals, checking out assigned reading and general books, door checking and shelving books.

1982 Summer: March Companies, Inc., Iowa City
Route Driver: Vacation relief driver; also filled in for terminated salesmen. Responsibilities included selling, delivering, accounting, banking, inventory control, and customer service.

1981 Summer: Karmond Lumber Co., Cedar Rapids
Customer Service: Assisted customers in filling their orders, trained new employees, stocked merchandise, took inventories, and made deliveries to customers' homes.

1980 Summer: Cambridge Condominiums, Cedar Rapids
Maintenance Person: Duties included landscaping and general maintenance.

HONORS AND ACTIVITIES
Dean's Honor List—Seven Terms
Volunteer Income Tax Assistance
Iowa State Finance Club Membership Director
Gamma Phi Nu Fraternity
Interfraternity Council Representative

THREE WELL-WRITTEN STATEMENTS DEMONSTRATING A BROAD RANGE OF EXPERIENCES.

WELL-PHRASED STATEMENTS THAT MAKE THE MOST OUT OF EACH POSITION.

DEMONSTRATES LEADERSHIP AND ACHIEVEMENT MOTIVATION.

A WELL-THOUGHT OUT RESUME THAT MAKES MAXIMUM USE OF THIS INDIVIDUAL'S OFFERINGS.

COMBINED

Resume Example #19: Fast-track creativity seeking career enhancement.

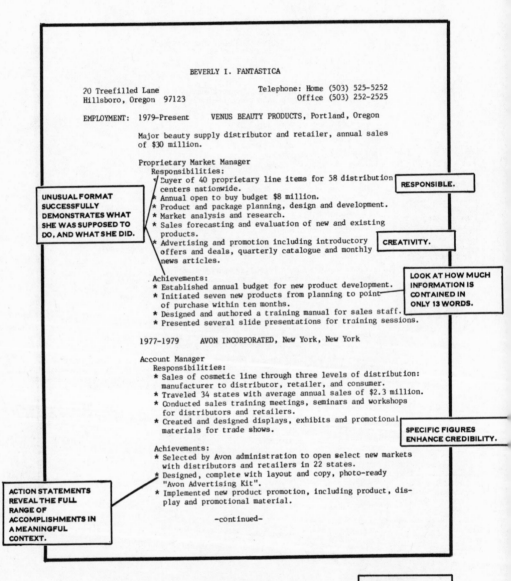

BEVERLY I. FANTASTICA

20 Treefilled Lane
Hillsboro, Oregon 97123

Telephone: Home (503) 525-5252
Office (503) 252-2525

EMPLOYMENT: 1979-Present   VENUS BEAUTY PRODUCTS, Portland, Oregon

Major beauty supply distributor and retailer, annual sales
of $30 million.

Proprietary Market Manager
Responsibilities:
* Buyer of 40 proprietary line items for 58 distribution
  centers nationwide.
* Annual open to buy budget $8 million.
* Product and package planning, design and development.
* Market analysis and research.
* Sales forecasting and evaluation of new and existing
  products.
* Advertising and promotion including introductory
  offers and deals, quarterly catalogue and monthly
  news articles.

Achievements:
* Established annual budget for new product development.
* Initiated seven new products from planning to point
  of purchase within ten months.
* Designed and authored a training manual for sales staff.
* Presented several slide presentations for training sessions.

1977-1979   AVON INCORPORATED, New York, New York

Account Manager
Responsibilities:
* Sales of cosmetic line through three levels of distribution:
  manufacturer to distributor, retailer, and consumer.
* Traveled 34 states with average annual sales of $2.3 million.
* Conducted sales training meetings, seminars and workshops
  for distributors and retailers.
* Created and designed displays, exhibits and promotional
  materials for trade shows.

Achievements:
* Selected by Avon administration to open select new markets
  with distributors and retailers in 22 states.
* Designed, complete with layout and copy, photo-ready
  "Avon Advertising Kit".
* Implemented new product promotion, including product, dis-
  play and promotional material.

-continued-

UNUSUAL FORMAT SUCCESSFULLY DEMONSTRATES WHAT SHE WAS SUPPOSED TO DO, AND WHAT SHE DID.

RESPONSIBLE.

CREATIVITY.

LOOK AT HOW MUCH INFORMATION IS CONTAINED IN ONLY 13 WORDS.

SPECIFIC FIGURES ENHANCE CREDIBILITY.

ACTION STATEMENTS REVEAL THE FULL RANGE OF ACCOMPLISHMENTS IN A MEANINGFUL CONTEXT.

CHRONOLOGICAL

BEAUTIFULLY ORGANIZED AND IMPRESSIVE.

Resume Example #19; page two

Page 2

Awards:
* Avon Sales of the Month Award (9 times).
* Best Sales Presentation Award: 1979.

THE TYPE OF AWARD
THAT GETS ATTENTION.

1974-1977   MANNEQUIN MODEL AGENCY, St. Claire Shores, Michigan

Licensed fashion and modeling school and agency.

Director of Education
  Responsibilities:
  * Researched, designed, and authored three curriculum programs.
  * Designed and authored training manual.
  * Trained, managed and supervised office and teaching staff.
  * Coordinated and conducted nearly 100 seminars and lectures
    to civic, education and business groups.

EDUCATION: 1974   OREGON COLLEGE, Medford, Oregon
             B.S., Fashion Merchandising and Marketing

SOLID ACADEMIC
CREDENTIALS.

FOREIGN
LANGUAGES: French, Spanish.

NO PERSONAL DETAILS
ABOUT MARITAL
OR FAMILY STATUS.

75

Resume Example #20: Transforming "housewifery" into job-related skills.

Lotta Toffer
327 Carmichele Avenue
Topeka, Kansas 66601
(913) 123-0000

Objective

A challenging position that will both utilize and strengthen the organizational and motivational skills acquired in over 11 years of diverse, demanding responsibilities.

> SOMEWHAT VAGUE, BUT WORTH INCLUDING.

Experience

Recently completed over 11 years as a suburban housewife and mother of three children, with success and skill in the following areas:

> POSITIVE STATEMENT TRANSLATING HOUSEWIFE FUNCTIONS AND EXPERIENCE INTO JOB-RELATED SKILLS.

* Budgeting--Accountable for the control and disbursement of an annual budget of $29,200.

* Prioritizing--Established schedules, met deadlines, and simultaneously coordinated several diverse tasks.

* Training and Supervision--Trained, instructed and directed three junior associates, whose development was under my jurisdiction, in a wide variety of skills (from bicycle riding to writing term papers to managing a paper route).

* Motivation and Influence--Developed marketing strategies and sold plans regarding personal development and goals clarification in the form of music lessons, soccer, computer classes, library research, museums, cultural events and art galleries.

> ACTION VERBS, IMPACT STATEMENTS.

* Recruitment, Interviewing, and Selection of Personnel--Hired a wide variety of professionals, including electricians, physicians, roofers, decorators and babysitters.

* Purchasing--Analyzed and initiated purchases of low-budget to high-ticket items, including 2 automobiles, 950 square yards of carpeting, 24-cubic-foot freezer, swim club membership, orthodontic and medical services, and 6 rooms of furniture.

Note: All the above was accomplished successfully; during this time, a 2-year Associate Degree was completed at Topeka Junior College, with membership on the Dean's List 5 out of 6 semesters.

> VALIDATES CLAIM TO MANAGEMENT SKILLS.

Excellent references available upon request.

FUNCTIONAL

> EMPHASIZES JOB-RELATED SKILLS AND ACHIEVEMENTS.

Resume Example #21: A legal specialist provides in-depth details.

LEON R. LAWLESS

40 Orchard Avenue
Ogden, UT 84404
(801) 866-1389

EXPERIENCE

NOTHING FANCY HERE; STRAIGHTFORWARD FACTS TELL IT ALL.

1981-present

WEDMAN, GIBBONS, GOLDMAN & MOORE
(1981 spin-off from Moran, Sullivan, Forrest & Yee)
Ogden, UT   ASSOCIATE ATTORNEY

TECHNICAL DETAILS LIKE THESE ARE REQUIRED FOR PROFESSIONS SUCH AS LAW.

Conduct all aspects of patent prosecution, including: patentability evaluations and validity opinions; evaluation of disclosure letters; disclosure interviews with inventors and counsel; preparation, filing and prosecution of patent applications relating to: silicon polymer chemistry and embodiments covering hard coatings; adhesives, non-stick coatings, silicone elastomers; production of hyperpure silicon; epoxy resins and curing agents; fiber resin matrix prepregs and composites; emulsion-based paints and coatings; ultraviolet light screening agents; high-temperature lubricants; thermoplatics; secondary oil recovery and transmission of liquid media; highway construction; refractory composites; steam generators; Examiner interviews; preparation of appeal briefs; oral argument before the Board of Appeals; preparation and prosecution of reissue applications. Responsible for preparation and prosecution of trademark applications, trademark appeals and oral argument before the TTAB, and trademark oppositions. Responsible for all pretrial aspects of patent and trademark litigations. Prepare confidential disclosure agreements, perform legal research and prepare legal memoranda.

1980-81

MORAN, SULLIVAN, FORREST & YEE
Provo, UT   ASSOCIATE ATTORNEY

Managed major aspects of patent prosecution and appeal, including: evaluation of disclosures; interviews with inventors and counsel; preparation, filing and prosecution of patent applications relating to: silicon hard coatings and vulcanizates; treated silica fillers; thermoplastics; wire enamels; frangible adhesive containers; patent litigation including drafting and responding to interrogatories, examination and control of documents and exhibits; organizing depositions; legal research and drafting legal memoranda.

page one

CHRONOLOGICAL

LEON R. LAWLESS   page two

1979-80	**HORVATH, SWEENEY & ARCHER** Salt Lake City, UT

Conducted project to analyze terms of over 12,000 license agreements and entertainment contracts, and creation of data base allowing comparison of same.

1972-77 (summers)	**BRIGHAM YOUNG UNIVERSITY,** Department of Biochemistry Lab Assistant

Supervised running of continuous, complex protein separation process; responsible for purifying, assaying and storing selected enzymes; developed mutant strains of *Pseudomonas* bacteria; maintained and harvested several bacterial cultures.

EDUCATION

J.D. 1979   **BRIGHAM YOUNG UNIVERSITY**
Equitas (BYLS newspaper) writer, summer intern in City Council President's Office

B.A. Biological   **BRIGHAM YOUNG UNIVERSITY**
Sciences
B.A. Psychology   Microbiology,
1976   Physiological Psychology

ADMISSIONS

United States Patent and Trademark Office
Bar of the State of Utah

MEMBERSHIPS

American Bar Association
Copyright Society of the U.S.A.
Utah Patent, Trademark and Copyright Law Association
Utah County Lawyers' Association

RELEVANT AND
NECESSARY TO THE
LEGAL PROFESSION.

Resume Example #22: A housewife with some earlier professional experience pulls it all together.

RAMONA REENTRY

1404 Marlboro
Minneapolis, Minnesota 55401

Work (612) 001-0011
Home (612) 100-1100

STRAIGHTFORWARD
JOB OBJECTIVE.

OBJECTIVE: Journalism: Financial / Economic / General News Reporting.

SIGNIFICANT ACCOMPLISHMENTS:

- Initiated, organized and successfully led PTA. Sponsored 1-year fund drive raising $36,250 (1979).
- Selected to 5-member Emment County Scholastic Achievement Board which distributes $50,000 in college scholarships to deserving, underprivileged high school seniors.
- Successfully organized 44-member petitioning group which led to tax referendum being placed on Emment County election — 1978.
- Chosen as one of four finalists for "Volunteer Citizen of the Year - 1981."
- Regular contributor to the National Scholastic Achiever, a quarterly journal. Have published 11 articles from 1981 to present.

CREATES A BUSY, EFFICIENT IMPRESSION OF SOMEONE WHO GETS THINGS DONE.

NOTEWORTHY.

EDUCATION:

- B.S. Journalism: University of Chicago, 1971. 3.4/4.0 GPA - Graduated "With Distinction."
- Post-graduate study: Illinois State University, 1975-1977. Economics and Finance - 8 classes at senior undergraduate level - 3.9/4.0 GPA.

DEMONSTRATES CONTINUATION OF ACTIVE INTERESTS.

PROFESSIONAL EXPERIENCE:

National Scholastic Achiever, 1981 - Present:
Part-Time (20 Hrs./Wk.) Position — Research, writing and office management.

Chicago Tribune, 1971 - 1973.
Special Events Reporter. Left voluntarily to raise family.

Excellent References Available Upon Request.

MAY BE IMPORTANT FOR SOMEONE NOT CURRENTLY EMPLOYED.

FUNCTIONAL

Resume Example #23: A retired executive seeking part-time consulting work.

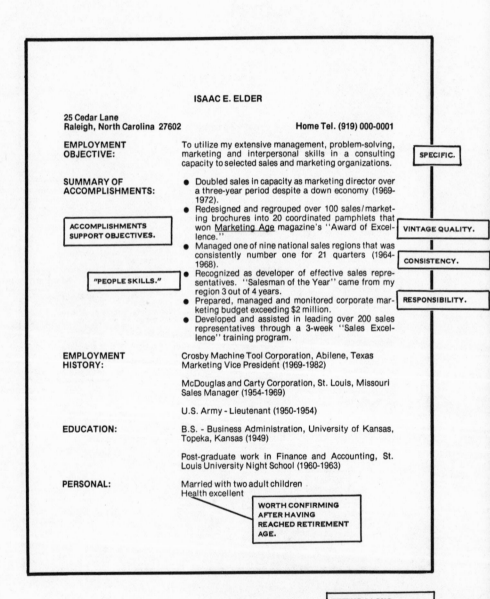

ISAAC E. ELDER

25 Cedar Lane
Raleigh, North Carolina 27602   **Home Tel. (919) 000-0001**

EMPLOYMENT OBJECTIVE:
To utilize my extensive management, problem-solving, marketing and interpersonal skills in a consulting capacity to selected sales and marketing organizations.

> SPECIFIC.

SUMMARY OF ACCOMPLISHMENTS:

> ACCOMPLISHMENTS SUPPORT OBJECTIVES.

> "PEOPLE SKILLS."

- Doubled sales in capacity as marketing director over a three-year period despite a down economy (1969-1972).
- Redesigned and regrouped over 100 sales/marketing brochures into 20 coordinated pamphlets that won <u>Marketing Age</u> magazine's "Award of Excellence."
- Managed one of nine national sales regions that was consistently number one for 21 quarters (1964-1968).
- Recognized as developer of effective sales representatives. "Salesman of the Year" came from my region 3 out of 4 years.
- Prepared, managed and monitored corporate marketing budget exceeding $2 million.
- Developed and assisted in leading over 200 sales representatives through a 3-week "Sales Excellence" training program.

> VINTAGE QUALITY.

> CONSISTENCY.

> RESPONSIBILITY.

EMPLOYMENT HISTORY:
Crosby Machine Tool Corporation, Abilene, Texas
Marketing Vice President (1969-1982)

McDouglas and Carty Corporation, St. Louis, Missouri
Sales Manager (1954-1969)

U.S. Army - Lieutenant (1950-1954)

EDUCATION:
B.S. - Business Administration, University of Kansas, Topeka, Kansas (1949)

Post-graduate work in Finance and Accounting, St. Louis University Night School (1960-1963)

PERSONAL:
Married with two adult children
Health excellent

> WORTH CONFIRMING AFTER HAVING REACHED RETIREMENT AGE.

COMBINED

> FITTING A LONG, SUCCESSFUL CAREER ONTO A BRIEF BUT POWERFUL PAGE.

Resume Example #24: Career enhancement on the middle-management level.

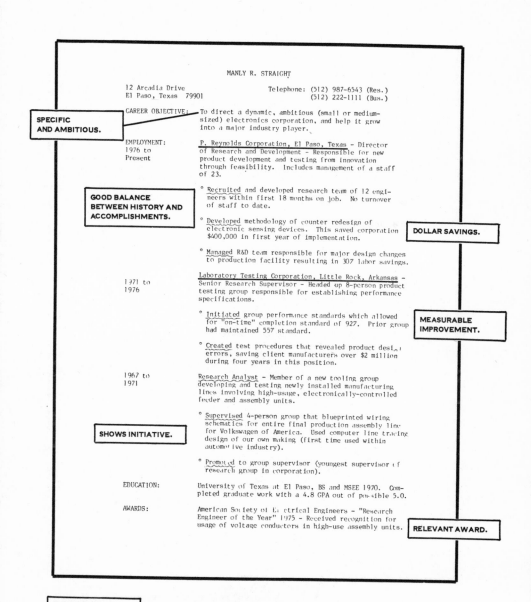

MANLY R. STRAIGHT

12 Arcadia Drive   Telephone: (512) 987-6543 (Res.)
El Paso, Texas 79901   (512) 222-1111 (Bus.)

SPECIFIC AND AMBITIOUS.

CAREER OBJECTIVE: To direct a dynamic, ambitious (small or medium-sized) electronics corporation, and help it grow into a major industry player.

EMPLOYMENT:
1976 to
Present

P. Reynolds Corporation, El Paso, Texas - Director of Research and Development - Responsible for new product development and testing from innovation through feasibility. Includes management of a staff of 23.

GOOD BALANCE BETWEEN HISTORY AND ACCOMPLISHMENTS.

° Recruited and developed research team of 12 engineers within first 18 months on job. No turnover of staff to date.

° Developed methodology of counter redesign of electronic sensing devices. This saved corporation $400,000 in first year of implementation.

DOLLAR SAVINGS.

° Managed R&D team responsible for major design changes to production facility resulting in 30% labor savings.

1971 to
1976

Laboratory Testing Corporation, Little Rock, Arkansas - Senior Research Supervisor - Headed up 8-person product testing group responsible for establishing performance specifications.

° Initiated group performance standards which allowed for "on-time" completion standard of 92%. Prior group had maintained 55% standard.

MEASURABLE IMPROVEMENT.

° Created test procedures that revealed product design errors, saving client manufacturers over $2 million during four years in this position.

1967 to
1971

Research Analyst - Member of a new tooling group developing and testing newly installed manufacturing lines involving high-usage, electronically-controlled feeder and assembly units.

° Supervised 4-person group that blueprinted wiring schematics for entire final production assembly line for Volkswagen of America. Used computer line tracing design of our own making (first time used within automotive industry).

SHOWS INITIATIVE.

° Promoted to group supervisor (youngest supervisor of research group in corporation).

EDUCATION: University of Texas at El Paso, BS and MSEE 1970. Completed graduate work with a 4.8 GPA out of possible 5.0.

AWARDS: American Society of Electrical Engineers - "Research Engineer of the Year" 1975 - Received recognition for usage of voltage conductors in high-use assembly units.

RELEVANT AWARD.

THIS RESUME SAYS A GREAT DEAL IN A RELATIVELY SMALL SPACE.

CHRONOLOGICAL

Resume Example #25: *Careful organization solves the problem of squeezing a lot of information onto two pages.*

ARTHUR D. ROSENBERG

000 West 00th Street
New York, N.Y. 10025

home: (212) 555-0000
office: (201) 222-1515

SUMMARY:

Over 20 years of professional accomplishments.

> THIS LETS US KNOW
> WHAT IS TO FOLLOW.

WRITER/EDITOR
Technical
Instructional
Advertising/Promotion

MANAGER/INSTRUCTOR
Training
Administration
Marketing/Sales

SPECIAL SKILLS

Solving problems: transforming incomplete or confusing technical and instructional materials into accurate, readable documentation.

> STRONG, CONFIDENT
> STATEMENT.

SOFTWARE

WordStar, DW 2, Multimate, Wang, IBM 38, TSO ISPF editor.

ACHIEVEMENTS

WRITER

> GOOD ACTION WORDS
> AND PHRASES.

- Currently documenting IDMS installation at Purolator Courier, including user manuals and instructional materials; conducting training programs for instructors.
- Created HELP screens for brokerage system on IBM 38.
- Documented implementation of payroll/personnel software system: functional specs and user manuals.
- Researched and wrote bank procedures on security systems, data collection/compilation for hardware/software productivity reports, and related areas.
- Created technical/instructional documentation for IMS (IBM-compatible) payroll/personnel system.
- Researched and wrote two published consumer-oriented studies on computer-based energy management systems.

EDITOR

- Published college math and business textbooks.
- Editor of monthly health care newsletter.
- Translated foreign language technical and promotional documentation for Winter Olympics (Grenoble).
- Edited user/technical documentation, instructional manuals, annual reports, catalogs, proposals.

MANAGER

- Established New York office for human resources firm.
- Supervised multinational staff at U.N. (Geneva).
- Second in charge of marketing activities for two international publishers of technical/educational materials.
- Consultant to U.S. Department of Education (OESE).

INSTRUCTOR

- Conducted classes and seminars at the following:
  Purolator Courier (N.J.)
  Union College (N.J.)
  Berlitz School (Paris)
  McGraw-Hill (N.Y.)
  University of Stockholm (Sweden)

COMBINED

> THE INITIAL DRAFT OF
> THIS RESUME COVERED
> 5½ PAGES. IT TOOK
> A LOT OF IMAGINATION
> AND REFLECTION TO
> GET IT DOWN TO
> A REASONABLE SIZE.

Resume Example #25; page two

**EMPLOYMENT
HISTORY**
1979 - Present

Recent Clients:

SUGGESTS THAT THERE
WERE EVEN MORE.

Purolator Courier	U.S. Department of Education
Paramount Pictures	Comerica - Detroit Bank
Morgan Guarantee	Paladyne Software Systems
RAVA Systems	Information Science
McGraw-Hill	Delmar Publishers

1975 - 1979   International Labor Office   ASSISTANT MANAGER,
Geneva, Switzerland   PUBLICATIONS

1973 - 1975   Dun Donnelley Publishing   EDITOR: BUSINESS
New York   & MATHEMATICS

1972 - 1973   Harcourt Brace Jovanovich   ASSISTANT MANAGER,
New York   PUBLICATIONS

1968 - 1972   McGraw-Hill Book Company   MARKETING MANAGER
New York

**PROFESSIONAL
ASSOCIATIONS**

ICCA — Independent Computer Consultants Association
The Authors Guild
The Authors League

RELEVANT
AFFILIATIONS.

EDUCATION

M.A., English, French — University of Grenoble, France
B.A., Psychology — University of California at L.A.

**FOREIGN
LANGUAGES**

French, Spanish, German, Italian, Dutch, Swedish

□ □ □

We're confident these widely divergent resumes have provided you with a format and some fresh ideas that will enable you to display your skills effectively. They will encourage the interviewer to spend more time studying your resume, and less time with the 244 others.

The successful resume is an art form. We don't want you to think of your resume as a potential minefield, where the slightest "mistake" can eliminate you from the running. As these samples demonstrate, there are countless ways to present your background in its most favorable light; there is, of course, no single "right" way. Follow the format in any of these resumes, or borrow from several; the choice is yours.

Now that you've seen some of the recommended methods, a look at some of the *wrong* ways of writing resumes may prove instructive (and, possibly, entertaining).

Chapter Five:
The 5 Worst Resumes We've Ever Seen

If a good resume is a work of art, a bad resume can be a masterpiece of self-destruction.

Included in this chapter are five of the worst resumes we've ever seer, selected from among those which we assume to have been honest (if misguided) attempts at interesting a potential employer. That they fail is obvious. We shall briefly point out some of their most poignant flaws, and how three of them could have been successfully rewritten.

RESUME   VINCENT VAGUELY

PERSONAL: Birth Date: February 25, 1959. Single.
                   Excellent health. Willing to travel and/or
                   relocate.

EDUCATION: B.S. in Business Administration, Central
                   Michigan University, with a major in finance,
                   24 credit hours; additional concentration
                   in marketing and economics. Overall GPA 3.1.
                   Date of graduation, May 7, 1981.

EXTRA-   Marketing Association, 1979, 1980, 1981.
CURRICULAR   Finance Club, 1980-81.
ACTIVITIES: Student Advisory Council, 1980-81.
                   Theta Chi Fraternity - Secretary, 1979-80
                                          Rush Chairman, 1980-81

INTERESTS,   Sports (golf, bowling, softball, basketball);
HOBBIES: leisure reading and music.

WORK   1977 - Warehouseman for Leaseway of Westland, MI
EXPERIENCE: 1978 - Warehouseman for Leaseway of Westland, 4I
                   1979 - Warehouseman for Leaseway of Westland, MI
                   1980 - Temporary Welding Inspector - Ford Motor
                          Company (after being laid off, painted
                          exteriors of homes).

ADDRESS: Home: 66666 Fox Glen
                         Farmington Hills, MI   48018
                         Phone: 313-666-0606
                                313-66'-0607

COMMENTS: I feel that I am a dependable, personable and
                   hard working individual who could be an asset
                   to your business.

NAME: VINCENT VAGUELY

Vincent Vaguely's vitae could (and maybe should) have been written on a 3-by-5 index card. This is the ideal size for recipes and other nonessentials. For although Vaguely feels he'd be an asset to our business, he has given us precious little data to support this optimistic view.

Now let's tear apart what Vincent Vaguely *did* include:

- *Resume:* Indeed, we know what it was intended to be, and so the label is superfluous.

- *Personal:* This information is unnecessary. If the writer insists on including it, he should have placed it at the very end.

- *Education:* Adequate, but poorly presented.

- *Extra-Curricular Activities:* Okay, but "Related Activities" might sound more grown up.

- *Interests, Hobbies:* Who cares?

- *Work Experience:* Should list the last job first. The same job need not be listed more than once. No mention is made of job responsibilities or accomplishments.

- *Address:* We finally discover where Vincent Vaguely lives. Of course, the address belongs up at the top.

- *Comments:* Unsubstantiated and unconvincing.

```
CHARLES "CHUCK" CONFUSER                    Telex: Smartashell
Easy Street
Big Town, NJ  07990

                    Statement of Position
                    As of July 20, 1985


                "U" are current unit valuations
                of relative worth to investor.


ASSETS
CURRENT ASSETS
Abilities Derived Through Current Major Classes
      Technical Capabilities                           U 55
      Spirit of competition (less allowance for cooperation)   90
      Communicative capacity                             90
      Background in business courses                    100
          Units from current major classes              335
Leadership and Decision Making Ability                  125
          TOTAL CURRENT ASSETS                          460
Health and Physical Attributes                          100
Former Education                                         75
Determination, Self-Confidence, and Self-Support (net of
      realization of dependence on others)              125
Goodwill and Intangibles                                100
TOTAL ASSETS                                          U 860



LIABILITIES AND STOCKHOLDERS EQUITY
CURRENT LIABILITIES
Amount Due Others for Maintenance of Interest and
      Self-Development                                 U 235
Amount Due Work Experience                              115
          TOTAL CURRENT LIABILITIES                     350
Long Term Debt to Supporters of Current Position        140
Debt Related to Mark 12:17                              110
TOTAL LIABILITIES                                       600
STOCKHOLDERS EQUITY
Common Stock                                             55
Retained Earnings -- To Facilitate Future Development   210
TOTAL LIABILITIES AND STOCKHOLDERS EQUITY             U 860
```

NAME: CHARLES "CHUCK" CONFUSER

Believe it or not, such resumes as this actually *do* turn up from time to time. Chuck has obviously confused numerical facility with imagination and cleverness. A potential employer would not. This is not to say that innovation and creativity are negative ingredients in resume-writing perforce. But they must be applied judiciously and intelligently so as to complement, not dominate, important and clearly-organized information.

This document not only is *not* a resume, it doesn't come close to fulfilling the *purpose* of a resume. Even if someone took the trouble to try and figure out the "formula" (bear in mind the other 244 resumes waiting on the interviewer's desk), it provides no comprehensible basis on which to evaluate the aspirant's experience or abilities.

The lesson here is that a resume should provide its readers with relevant information; it shouldn't test their patience.

And if all of this were not enough, the use of a nickname is another "no-no."

Eleanora Unsura
1404 Moore Ave.
Lincoln, MO 65438
(417) 471-1174
Social Sec. No. 390-92-6649

Level of Education:
High School Harper Woods High School 4 years
Business School Hallmark Business Machines Institute 9 months
Course of study Computer Programming
Specialization Cobol & RPGII Languages
Career Objective To Work Hard and become a good Programmer
Possible Salary $10,000 to $20,000 a year
Employment Experience:
Present Employer Whall Security Corp.
Job Title Security Officer.
Date of Employment 12/27/78. Current Salary $4.24 an hour
Job Responsibility To Take care of clients properity from Fire
or Theft.
Previous Employer Little Caecars Inc.
Job Title Store manager & pizza maker
Dates of Employment March, 1978 to November, 1978 Salary $180 a
week.
Job Responsibility To make pizzas when busy and to do daily
paper work.
Personal References: Billy and Jane Smith, 1403 Moore Ave. (a-
cross the street).

                                    Truly Yours,
                                    Eleanora Unsura
                                    Eleanora Unsura

NAME: ELEANORA UNSURA

What's wrong with this little monstrosity? Almost everything, alas. The major flaws are that it is grammatically abhorrent, poorly punctuated, full of misspellings, and unpleasing to the eye. It goes on to flout, destroy, or merely ignore the fundamental rules of writing a successful resume.

To mention just a few specifics, salaries (past, present, and requested) should *never* appear upon a resume. Nor should references, or jobs like "pizza maker." If you insist on such references, at least spell the name of your employer correctly. Finally, Eleanora's resume doesn't give the interviewer a chance to think about her background. There is no open space, relevancies and irrelevancies are intermingled, and it is completely lacking in structure.

Ms. Unsura gives us no idea of what she may have to offer a potential employer. She would be well-advised to solicit help in organizing and writing a resume with purpose and technique!

On the following page, we offer an alternative:

ELEANORA UNSURA

1404 Moore Avenue   Telephone: 417/471-1174
Lincoln, Missouri 65338

OBJECTIVE: A programming position allowing for professional
                        skill development, multiple applications, and
                        potential for career growth.

EMPLOYMENT   Whall Security Corporation - Security Officer
HISTORY: Provide security service to a variety of business
1978 - Present   clients - hospitals to manufacturing concerns.

                        * Uncovered electrical fire in early stages while
                          on patrol at Parkcrest Hospital, resulting in
                          quick and easy smothering of fire and saving
                          potential loss of costly research equipment.

                        * Maintained perfect attendance record while em-
                          ployed at Whall, despite working at least 30+
                          hours/week and completing coursework at Hallmark.

                        * "Employee of the Month" - Recipient 7 times.

1978   Little Caesar's Incorporated - Store Manager
                        Managed $515,000 annual receipt, 7-employee carry-
                        out restaurant.

                        * Reduced losses from incorrectly filled orders by
                          redesigning order form. This resulted in a 55%
                          drop in losses.

                        * Appointed manager at age 17 and while still a
                          senior in high school.

EDUCATION: Hallmark Business Machine Institute - 1982.
                        Completed 9-month program with a proficiency score
                        on final testing of 92%.

                        Cape Harris H.S., 1978. Graduated within College
                        Preparatory Curriculum.

ACTIVE   Home computers, computer techrical journals.
INTERESTS:

94

It's difficult to believe, but this is the same Eleanora Unsura that authored the previous interviewer's nightmare. With some careful thought given to her achievements, a newfound respect for the English language, some carefully-chosen action verbs, and a format which would save the employer from a headache, Eleanora's resume has made a Pygmalion-like transition.

RESUME

I.M. Brusk   Department of Geography
123 S. Adams   California State University
Correl, California 91106   80 State College Avenue
(213) 000-0000   Fullerton, California 91106
                                     (213) 000-0001

EDUCATION

1979 - present	School of Business Administration & Economics	
	California State University-Fullerton	M.B.A.
1968 - 1972	Economic Geography Option	
	U.C. Berkeley	Ph.D.
1965 - 1968	Geography, Major - Economics, Minor	B.A.
	University of Bristol (England)	Special Honors

WORK EXPERIENCE

1976 - present   Associate Professor
                 Department of Geography
                 California State University-Fullerton

1972 - 1976   Assistant Professsor
                 Department of Geography
                 California State University-Fullerton

1971 - 1972   Instructor
                 Department of Economics
                 University of San Francisco

CONSULTING

1978 - 1984   Urban Econometrics Co., Fullerton, Ca.

1978 - 1981   Market Profiles, Inc., Tustin, Ca.

1978   Orange County Forecast and Analysis Center

AWARDS, HONORS

1969 - 1970   James P. Sutton Fellowship, U.C. Berkeley

1968 - 1969   Thomas and Elizabeth Williams Scholarship,
                 Glamorgan City Council

1965 - 1968   Special Honors, University of Bristol

NAME: I.M. BRUSK

What a pity to have amassed such an impressive record of academic excellence and to portray it in such an unimpressive fashion.

This resume tells us that I.M. Brusk has earned an MBA, a PhD, and special honors. We can further deduce, with careful study, that the individual was promoted from Assistant to Associate Professor.

The rest is speculation. Has this apparently intelligent person published? What courses and seminars has he taught? What are his academic and scientific specialties? What was the nature of his consulting? Has he any noteworthy research in progress? What, if any, are his goals? Why, we don't even know if he is, in fact, a *he* or a *she*.

Presumably, Professor Brusk is looking for a highly specialized position. But there are other qualified people out there with PhDs and honors of their own in competition. Given similar academic credentials, those whose resumes present them in a more interesting light are likelier to get the interview.

Our advice to I.M. Brusk is to rewrite this resume with the elements we've outlined in *The Resume Handbook*. It might look something like the one on the next page.

ISABELLA M. BRUSK

123 South Adams
Correl, California 91106

Residence: 213/000-0000
Work: 213/000-0000

EXPERIENCE

1972 - Current   California State University - Fullerton, Associate Professor, Department of Geography. Responsible for curriculum development for entire department covering 3,700 students annually. Personally direct 10 department classes each year, including newly-designed class entitled "Changing Weather Patterns - Dawn of a New Age."

- Co-authored "Economic Cycle Influences of Changing Political Boundaries", a highly-acclaimed series of articles appearing in July-October 1984 issues of the *Research Economist*.

Selected as:

- Member of Governor's Council on Earthquake Readiness, a 16-member task force of business, academic and government people assessing current state readiness regarding safety, economic disruption and proposed construction considerations. Youngest member of panel.
- Rated 96.4 out of 100 by nearly 750 students attending my classes during 1972-84. "90" is considered "outstanding."
- Developed and tested computer model identifying economic trends (i.e., unemployment rates, median incomes, others) caused by changing populations. This was accomplished during a consulting assignment with Urban Econometrics, Fullerton, California.
- Conceived, designed and sold predictive voting model that pinpoints political voting trends utilizing demographics rather than polling. This predictive model has accurately predicted 27 out of 29 county races in 1979-82.

1971 - 1972   University of San Francisco, Instructor - Department of Economics. Responsible for leading one senior-level undergrad and two graduate-level Microeconomics classes involving 120 + students.

- Developed instructional curriculum for 60-hour class entitled "Economic Patterns and Their Historical Perspectives."

page 2

PROFESSIONAL ASSOCIATION
American Association of Geographers

LANGUAGES
Welsh, French

PUBLICATIONS
1. Hydrological Implications of Geothermal Developments in the Imperial Valley of Southern California
    G. George, R.H. Foster, and D.K. Todd
    Sea Water Conversion Laboratory, UCB, Richmond, November, 1971.

2. 1974 Population Estimates
    G. George and G. Britton
    Report on the Status of Orange County, 1974. Working Document No. 1, Forecast and Analysis Center, Orange County, CA.

3. The Frequency of Social Contacts within a Time-Space Framework.
    G. George
    Submitted for publication.

PROFESSIONAL PAPERS
1. Intra-urban Interaction and Time-Space Budgets.
    G. George, D. Shimarua, and P. Barry
    Association of American Geographers, New Orleans, 1978.

2. The Soviet Concept of Optimal City Size
    G. George and C. Zumbrunnen
    Association of American Geographers, New Orleans, 1978.

EDUCATION
- Ph.D. - University of California at Berkeley, 1972.
  Economic Geography Option
- M.B.A. - California State University - Fullerton, 1982.
- B.A. - University of Bristol (England), 1968.
  Geography Major; Economics Minor. Graduated with honors.

We now know not only that Dr. Brusk is a *she,* but we've also gained a wealth of important information omitted from her initial resume. We've learned about her areas of expertise, that she has published extensively, and that she's popular with her students. Dr. Brusk, we find, has been appointed to a government panel; she is familiar with state-of-the-art techniques (computer modeling), and she has had consulting positions with private firms (no "bookish academic," *this* Dr. Brusk). Without any exaggeration, she has turned a limp and lifeless resume into one that will demand its share of recognition in a fiercely competitive market.

□ □ □

```
                              RESUME
                                OF
                         BART BRAMBLEBUSH

RESIDENCE:                                 OFFICE:
808 Hopkins Drive East                     Graduate School of Business
Windsor, Ontario                              Administration
                                           The University of Windsor
                                           Windsor, Ontario


PROFESSIONAL EXPERIENCE:
      1976          The University of Windsor
       to           Windsor, Ontario
     Present

                    1982        Director of Placement
                     to         Graduate School of Business Administration
                   Present

                    1980        Director, BBA Internship Program
                     to         Dearborn, Michigan Campus
                    1982

      1974          Substitute Teacher
       to           Windsor Public Schools
      1976          Windsor, Ontario

      1969          Training Manager
       to           Hespin & Marquette
      1974          Windsor, Ontario

      1966          Home Economics Teacher
       to           Weaton Public Schools
      1969          Weaton, Ontario


EDUCATION:
University of Windsor       Master of              Major:
Windsor, Ontario       Business Administration  Industrial Relations
                               1978

University of Buffalo       Bachelor of Science      Major:
Buffalo, New York               1962              Secondary Education

EXCELLENT REFERENCES AVAILABLE UPON REQUEST
```

NAME: BART BRAMBLEBUSH

The preceding resume is probably the most frequent, and thus typical, form of resume failure we've encountered. At first glance, it may not seem so bad. In fact, you may be saying, "Gee, that looks like mine!"

Indeed, Bramblebush's offering is not as obviously awful as some of the preceding examples of bad resumes. Its failure is more subtle and insidious, which is why we consider it more dangerous than the others. The problem isn't what we *see*, but rather what we don't.

At second glance, this sad excuse for a resume might be better suited to the epitaph etched in stone above his bones once Bart's career is terminated — it offers little more than the stuff of which memories are made. What — if anything — has Bart accomplished in his profession? Has he met with any noteworthy success? There must be *something* he has done over the years to interest a potential employer, but we certainly can't find it underneath his name.

Other than where Bramblebush has been, and when, this document provides job titles, identifies itself as his resume, and gratuitously promises good references to anyone who might be interested. Fortunately, we know Bart well enough to help him out of his predicament, and so we took the time to rewrite his chrono-illogical attempt into a solid resume. This version follows. Read both versions, and ask yourself if they appear to describe the same person.

BARTHOLOMEW B. BRAMBLEBUSH

808 Hopkins Lane Drive   Residence (519) 101-0001
Windsor, Ontario 74R 01S   Business   (519) 010-1000

PROFESSIONAL OBJECTIVE
    Attainment of a managerial level position as a Programs Director,
Project Manager or Section Head within a major university where
my array of administrative, analytic, planning and leadership
skills can be fully utilized.

EDUCATION
    M.B.A., University of Windsor, Windsor, Ontario-1978. Concen-
tration in Industrial Relations.

    B.A., University of Buffalo, Buffalo, New York-1966. Major in
Secondary Education.

SIGNIFICANT EXPERIENCE
    MANAGERIAL – Successfully headed 12-member, $540,000 annual
budget placement function; increased enrollments 114% over last
4 years at a 9000-student university.

    SYSTEMS DEVELOPMENT – Conceptualized and implemented computer-
ized records system projected to save $175,000 in administrative
expenses over next 3 years.

    FUNDS DEVELOPMENT – During 2-year assignment as BBA Internship
Program Director: established 359 successful corporate relation-
ships totaling 577 students, resulting in additional bottom-line
impact to university of $205,000.

    PROGRAM DESIGN – Originated and initiated Student Enrollment
Campaign involving promotional literature, student contacts at
high schools and junior colleges, and direct mail: resulted in
increase in enrollment during 1983 of 660 over 1982.

    TRAINING DESIGN – Designed Comprehensive Management Program
affecting 275 individuals covering all phases of management
from planning to controlling for major Canadian retailer.

    TEACHING EXCELLENCE – Runner up two years in row (1968-69) as
Teacher of the Year in a school district with 150 high school
teachers.

POSITIONS
    1976 – Present   Director of Placement, University of Windsor,
                    Windsor, Ontario   (1980-Present).

                    Director of BBA Internship Programs, University
                    of Windsor (1976-80).

    1974 – 1976   Substitute Teacher, Windsor Public Schools.

    1969 – 1974   Training Manager, Hespin & Marquette Ltd.,
                    Windsor, Ontario.

    1966 – 1969   Home Economics Teacher, Weaton Public Schools,
                    Weaton, Ontario.

Unlike Bart's first resume, his second shows that his flatly-stated job titles were accompanied by significant managerial, fiscal, teaching, and operational responsibilities. In the first resume, his job progression seems sketchy and undefined. The improved version informs us of a logical progression toward the position he is seeking. Bart's (Bartholomew's, rather) second resume is an interview-getter.

□ □ □

Without belaboring the point, even losing resumes can be transformed into winners. All you need are several hours of honest reflection (armed, of course, with your "resume tools"), an awareness of how your background can make you valuable to a potential employer, and a quick review of the basic resume guidelines outlined in chapter two. The rest is personal: choosing the format, typestyle, and layout that you feel best suits your background, while avoiding the pitfalls of poor resume writing.

Except for the brief final chapter on resume layout and design, this is our final word on successful resumes. The examples we have given you will hopefully provide the tools you need for your own, *unique* profile.

However, this is not the end of *The Resume Handbook*. In the next two chapters, we will focus on the two essential resume companions: the cover letter, and the personal sales (or broadcast) letter.

Chapter Six:
Cover Letters

Now that your resume is a polished gem, at least half the battle has been waged. It's time to hone a tool that lends your resume direction and appeal. You need a cover letter. After all, the potential employer, opening hundreds of resumes and letters daily, isn't going to know what to do with just a lonely resume.

Writing effective cover letters is often underestimated in the overall scheme of seeking a new job. But cover letters can be the important key to the right doors.

Take the one on the following page, for instance:

April 18, 1985

Arthur C. Reese
President
Southwest Tooling Research, Inc.
200 Mountain View Blvd.
Santa Fe, New Mexico 80801

Dear Mr. Reese:

Enclosed please find my resume. After reviewing it,
I am sure you will find that I'm a worthwhile and capable
professional engineer who deserves further attention.

My current situation no longer offers me the challenge
and responsibility level I demand. Because of this,
I feel it is time to seek out another opportunity.

If there is any interest in my capabilities, you can
reach me at 417/231-4414. I'm positive you will find
the time you spend analyzing my capabilities well worth
your time.

Sincerely,

Ann Carmichael

Ann Carmichael

Would you go on to read the attached resume if you received hundreds of similar documents each week? We doubt it. The letter leaves a lot to be desired: it fails to include vital information, lacks a definite purpose, and simply doesn't entice the recipient to read more.

Effective cover letters convey a sense of purpose. They project an air of enthusiasm — regarding both the writer and the company for which the writer wants to work. And they demonstrate the writer's understanding of the company's goals, either by supporting or challenging them.

OBJECTIVES OF THE COVER LETTER

A well-written cover letter satisfies the following objectives:

● It offers the job seeker an opportunity to personalize and target the resume to a particular person

● It allows the writer to direct particular attention to specific skills that may be important to the reader

● It enables the applicant to clearly state why this organization is of interest to him or her

● It opens the door for further communication and follow-through

Let's examine each of these points in depth:

□ *Personalization:* The personalized aspect of a cover letter is one of its major strengths. A resume, by its very nature, is impersonal. When mailed without a personalized cover letter, a resume may create the impression that the addressee is merely one of several random stops along the campaign trail.

Always address the cover letter to a specific individual within the target organization, preferably to the person who appears most likely to have decision-making authority for the position sought. Sales candidates should address the sales or marketing officer, while engineers are advised to approach the director of engineering. Any well-stocked library will have a variety of research aids such as trade journals, Standard & Poor's *Register of Corporations, Directors, and Executives,* Dun & Bradstreet's *Million Dollar Directory,* and many other research sources. Solid research results in a list of specific individuals within target organizations. It allows the writer to avoid the ill-advised heading: "To Whom It May Concern." If you aren't sure, call the company to verify your target's name and title; this is probably the best way to obtain the names you want.

☐ *Directing Attention to a Skill:* The ultimate question that job seekers must answer throughout their search is, "What can you do for us?" Its importance during the prospecting phase should not be overlooked. The cover letter allows the job seeker to highlight or draw attention to a particular skill or accomplishment that has meaning to the organization in question. That skill may or may not be included in the resume. Its inclusion in the cover letter, however, communicates some important information: that the writer has researched the company, identified the company's needs, and can fulfill those needs. In short, it says, "Here I am, the employee you've been waiting for!"

☐ *Clear Statement Indicating Reason for Interest:* This objective is the flip side of the above. Whereas before the writer highlighted a specific skill, here he or she is indicating where in the target organization this skill can best be put to use. The applicant is, once again, reinforcing the image of being knowledgeable and industry-wise.

☐ *Control and Follow-through:* This objective allows the job seeker to initiate the exchange of further communication. Much of the job search process lies outside the applicant's control. At least some control, however, is created when the applicant mails (and follows up) a resume and cover letter.

The applicant (assertively and diplomatically) determines *who* is doing *what* and *when.* The *who* in this case is the job seeker taking the initiative; *what* refers to future action; *when* is of the writer's choosing. The objective is to give the reader ample time to receive the cover letter and resume and to digest their contents, so the writer is a known entity when personal contact is established.

Now that the objectives of the cover letter have been brought into focus, let's return to the opening example and analyze its content.

With the exception of being personalized and staying within the recommended length of 200 words, this cover letter accomplishes relatively little. The sentence offering an explanation of the writer's current situation and why she wants to seek other employment is neither appropriate nor helpful. (The title of the bestselling book, *Never Complain, Never Explain* by Victor Lasky, represents a critical element to avoid within the cover letter: complaints and explanations.) The letter's style and tone evoke the average book on resumes and cover letters, which *The Resume Handbook* will show you how to avoid.

On the following page is one way the original letter might have been reworded:

April 25, 1985

Mr. Arthur C. Reese
President
Southwest Tooling Research, Inc.
200 Mountain View Blvd.
Santa Fe, New Mexico 80801

Dear Mr. Reese:

I read with great interest a recent article in
Engineering Today entitled "Southwest Tooling's Push
to Maintain Engineering Excellence." The article
talked of your plans to increase your Engineering
Research Lab Team. This emphasis on expansion appears
to be a positive sign of Southwest's continuing dedi-
cation to quality service. I am extremely intrigued
by the team research concept you have developed. The
motivating force within a research team offers each
member a sense of pride and accomplishment.

The enclosed resume demonstrates my extensive, long-
range commitment to tooling research. You will also
notice my own experience working with the team research
concept. It goes without saying that you are looking for
the best possible people to staff your growing organization.
I feel I can offer you and Southwest Tooling substantial
experience and the high degree of excellence you need.

I look forward to getting together to discuss your
open position. I will call you during the early part of
the week beginning March 22, to arrange an interview and
to discuss my possible involvement with Southwest Tooling.

Sincerely,

Ann Carmichael

Ann Carmichael

This version puts all four major objectives to use, stressing the writer's strengths and value (tooling research and team experience) to the reader. It answers the two important questions: "Why are you sending us your resume?" and, "What value can you offer us?" The length remains within the recommended maximum of 200 words, and the letter closes with the promise to follow up with a phone call. The overall tone is enthusiastic and informative, without being wordy or overstated. It is, all in all, a well-written cover letter. Another good example follows on the next page:

October 28, 1985

Mr. Robert T. McPhall
Vice President of Marketing
Lencor Industries, Incorporated
2002 Island Harbor
Fort Myers, Florida 20114

Dear Mr. McPhall:

I recently reviewed with interest an article you wrote in Sales Management magazine, entitled "Motivation Through Marketing Excellence." The marketing philosophy at Lencor corresponds to what I have accomplished on a smaller scale on my current assignment.

As you will note from my enclosed resume, my sales and marketing accomplishments, especially at Eastern General, favorably fit your "Marketplace Management" concept.

Because of my familiarity with your customer base and distribution network, I feel comfortable about my potential contribution to your growing organization. My experience over the last three years of increasing sales in my territory by 31% demonstrates my ability to succeed.

I will be in Fort Myers during the third and fourth weeks of November. May we sit down and discuss "Marketplace Management" and my strong interest in your sales group? I will contact you the first week in November to finalize arrangements.

I look forward to meeting with you.

Sincerely,

William J. Adamson
William J. Adamson

Once again, note how each of the four objectives is met with a forceful and energetic style. The writer has zeroed in on his value and how it relates to the employer's needs. His approach is interesting and flattering without exaggeration. He highlights areas of his resume that are clearly oriented toward the job he's seeking, demonstrates a knowledge of the industry, and takes the initiative by stating when he intends to call.

A cover letter is essential to the job search. Its effectiveness depends on understanding the objectives outlined here. A cover letter may not land the job, but it will certainly influence how favorably your resume is viewed. It may even determine whether your resume is viewed at all.

Chapter Seven:
Personal Sales Letters

The personal sales letter concept is too important to leave out of a comprehensive guide to writing resumes. Not to be confused with cover letters, which serve to introduce and accompany resumes, the personal sales letter (or "broadcast" letter) is a *substitute* for a resume. It is primarily used when writing to selected "cold prospects," rather than applying for announced openings through employment agencies, classified ads, and the like.

Because the emphasis of *The Resume Handbook* is on resumes, this section is intended as no more than an introductory guide to writing successful personal sales letters. Neverthless, the authors have researched and summarized the topic with a great degree of care. We hope you find this brief synopsis helpful.

PHILOSOPHY OF THE PERSONAL SALES LETTER

The purpose of a personal sales letter is to offer an alternative to confronting the reader with "yet another resume." In addition, it allows you to tailor your experience to the precise specifications of the position and the company to which you are applying. This approach is more commonly used by individuals writing to a large number of corporations where they hope to motivate the interest of a key decision-maker, and to explore the possibility of a current or future opening. It is less often employed when answering advertisements or announced openings, especially where formal resumes have been requested.

Like resumes, personal sales letters are intended to obtain an interview. They are, however, better suited to exploring corporate needs that may not yet have been defined. Personal sales letters are thus better suited to seeking executive rather than entry-level positions.

GENERAL GUIDELINES

Always direct your personal sales letter to a specific individual, not to the "Director," "Vice President," or other nameless title. If possible, avoid "Personnel" or "Employee Relations" departments, for they are generally oriented toward existing vacancies only. You can find the names of key decision-makers in the companies to which you plan to write in such directories as *The Directory of Directories; The National Job Bank; Million Dollar Directory;* Standard & Poor's *Register of Corporations, Directors, and Executives; Thomas Register of American Manufacturers; College Placement Annual;* and numerous other professional and industrial resources available at most libraries.

Your own profession may have a published directory — check the library if you are uncertain. A better alternative, though, is to phone the company and ask who is in charge of the department or section in which you're interested. Incidentally, you should also call to verify the names in all but the most up-to-date directories, for such listings quickly become obsolete.

Use standard business-sized stationery, preferably personalized. Type "PRIVATE AND CONFIDENTIAL" on the front of the envelope, or a secretary might open the letter and automatically pass it along to the personnel department, which is likely to negate your purpose.

Do not refer to specific past or current employers, and leave out any mention of current, past, or desired salary. Keep careful notes on all correspondence; be sure you have a quick, efficient way to locate a specific file when someone to whom you've written calls unexpectedly.

CONTENT OF THE PERSONAL SALES LETTER

☐ *Opening Paragraph*

Your opening paragraph is the attention-grabber; it must capture the reader's curiosity and entice him or her to continue reading. Unusual, intriguing information related to your objectives is a solid bet:

- "I increased the output of my department 212% while reducing manpower hours."

- "I made a successful living in South America for 7 years by selling African coffee in Brazil."

- "As R&D Director of a major manufacturer of electronic testing instruments, I initiated the development of four highly-regarded products."

- "How often does one have the opportunity to engage the services of an account executive who recently captured a $1.5 million contract from a giant competitor?"

- "My professors referred to my final MBA project in financial modeling (just completed) as 'brilliant' and 'innovative.' One of them suggested that an organization of your prominence in the industry could certainly make use of an honors graduate like myself, following graduation this coming June."

□ *Second Paragraph*

The second paragraph tells the reader why you are writing him or her. It identifies the specific job you're aiming for, concentrating on a single, carefully-researched objective:

- "This letter is intended to introduce me and to explore your potential need for a bilingual petroleum engineer who is quite willing to relocate. If you do happen to be looking for someone with my qualifications . . ."

- "I am writing because I anticipated you might have need of someone with my unusual blend of qualifications in biomedical marketing research. Should this be the case . . ."

- "My purpose in contacting you directly is to inquire whether you anticipate a need for an executive recruiter with a good deal of experience in the academic publishing industry. If so . . ."

□ *Third Paragraph*

This paragraph is calculated to create a desire for what you have to offer. You may state what you've accomplished in the field in question, or list similar functions that support the kind of job you're seeking. Describe outstanding achievements (from your resume) which directly support the job objective. Use short, direct sentences. Avoid imprecise adjectives like "incredible" or "terrific." Cite specific figures. Don't hesitate to say:

- "I accomplished/achieved/succeeded in . . ."

- "I have received six patents, with 11 pending, on . . ."

- "I saved my company $3.2 million by reducing . . ."

- "As Director of Marketing of a small company, I increased sales by . . ."

- "My architectural design was selected and, under my direction, implemented . . ."

□ *Fourth Paragraph*

State specific, positive facts about your education and other qualifications that can be verified. Include dates only if they are potentially useful to you:

- "MS (with honors) in Management from the University of Michigan. I majored in Personnel Relations, and minored in Industrial Psychology."

- "In 1985, I passed the 10th (final) actuarial exam for New York State."

- "I authored the 120-page 'Guide to XYZ Information Retrieval' (published by XYZ, Inc., 1985)."

□ *Fifth Paragraph*

The final paragraph tells the addressee what action you suggest on his or her part, or what may be expected from you. Let them know when and where you can be conveniently contacted:

- "It would be my pleasure to offer you additional details regarding my qualifications during an interview. You can reach me most evenings and weekends at the above number. I am looking forward to hearing from you at your earliest convenience.''

- ● ''I hope to hear from you prior to June 1, at which date I am expected to make a decision as to whether I will remain . . .''

- ● ''I plan to be in Chicago the week of February 2-6. In the event that you would like to arrange an interview during this period, you can reach me at my home (212/123-4567) after 6:30 most evenings throughout the month of January.''

Then sign the letter.

To further familiarize you with personal sales letters, two well-written examples follow. Note that they are both one-page documents, a length we regard as preferable, but not absolutely mandatory. We do, however, consider anything over a page-and-a-half as treading on very dangerous ground.

□ □ □

CAROLE CORRAL
133 Charter Boulevard
Berkley, Michigan 48077

Mr. James Masterson
President
Romar Corporation
3303 Euclid
Cleveland, Ohio 44114

Dear Mr. Masterson:

Employed as a Personnel Representative for an international,
medium-sized insurance company, I assisted in the development of
the corporate personnel department. By utilizing a centralized
system of recruiting, interviewing, and selection procedures,
I reduced turnover 30% over an 18-month period.

I am writing to you because your company may be in need of a
personnel professional with my two plus years of experience,
education, and training. If so, you may be interested in some of
my accomplishments:

* Researched and wrote a comprehensive, 88-page employee
  handbook which included corporate policies and employee
  benefits.

* Wrote corporate salary and wage policy, conducted salary
  surveys, and prepared and updated job descriptions.

* Administered company benefits including insurance and
  retirement programs for exempt and non-exempt personnel.
  Maintained effective verbal and written communications
  with insurance underwriters for revision and coordination
  of medical benefits.

* Responsible for collecting and reporting data on turnover,
  salary administration, EEO, and pension programs.

* Wrote a comprehensive employee training manual for a nonprofit health care facility which was distributed nationally
  to other health centers.

I received my BS in Management with a concentration in Human
Resources Management from Oakland University. I seek a challenge
and an opportunity where I can learn and advance within the personnel
field.

It would be a pleasure to review my qualifications with you in a
personal interview at your convenience. You can reach me after 5 p.m.
at 414/528-0280. I look forward to the opportunity to discuss career
opportunities with you.

Sincerely,

Carole Corral
Carole Corral

EDWARD EDWARDS
921 Marshbank Road
Marshall, Idaho 09117

Mr. William Tell
General Manager
MacIntosh Engineering
1400 Comstock
Mahwah, New Jersey 08108

Dear Mr. Tell:

In the last 35 months, I have successfully designed, installed, and made operational a computer-controlled, visually-activated robotics system. This system has already saved my firm $275,000, with additional second year savings anticipated to be nearly $560,000.

I am writing to you at this time because of my strong interest in your robotics efforts, especially in visual scanning applications. Your pioneering research compliments mine and has prompted me to contact your organization. Permit me to list some additional accomplishments:

★ Received the John A. Cartwright Award as Research Engineer of the Year, Stamford, Connecticut Chapter.

★ Published article: "Light Shading Activators in Visual Sensing Devices", Journal of Electrical Engineers, December 1983.

★ As Director of Research, 1981, improved on-time completion of scheduled projects 39% my first year, thereby saving $135,000 in early bid placements.

★ Successfully turned around an historically mismanaged, unprofitable production facility within 18 months; turned a net profit, reduced 50% plus turnover record in half, and cu: absenteeism by 61%.

★ Redesigned three major assembly lines, reducing downtime by 115%, reducing scrap by 55%, and improving product quality by 35%. An independent audit firm has conservatively estimated bottom line impact of these redesigns at $2.2 million.

I received my MSEE from Boston University, where I graduated with honors from their night program in 1976.

It would be a pleasure to offer you additional details on how I may contribute to your efforts in engineering and robotics research. You may contact me after 7 p.m. at home (208/123-4567). I look forward to your early call.

Yours truly,

Edward Edwards

Edward Edwards

□ □ □

The lessons from these two examples can be applied to personal sales letters in every profession. Personal sales letters allow you to highlight elements of your background in a more personalized format, and to stand slightly apart from the more traditional approaches.

Used alone, or in conjunction with a resume and cover letter, this technique may prove surprisingly effective if the simple guidelines we've outlined are followed carefully.

Chapter Eight:
Resume Design & Layout

It's no less important that your resume be pleasing to the eye than for it to clearly present the facts of your job history. People need to breathe while talking, otherwise their words would flow into a monotonic blend of syllables. The interviewer or potential employer reading your resume needs time to let his or her eye "breathe," a chance to pause and digest the achievements you're presenting.

This chapter will serve as a brief guide to structuring a resume that is physically appealing and complementary to your background.

The first thing to consider is the paper on which your resume (and accompanying cover letter, or solo personal sales letter) will be printed. An off-white paper stock may help your resume stand out in a pile, but beware of using pastels or darker colors, which look unprofessional. White standard business-sized stationery, of course, is always acceptable. Your resume should attract attention because of your carefully-worded achievements, not the paper you use.

As we cautioned earlier, try to limit your resume to a single page unless you have several years of experience and a diversity of noteworthy achievements. The interviewer will appreciate it.

The next thing to consider is the method you use to put your resume on paper. You have three basic choices: typesetting, typing, or word processing.

Modern photocomposition typesetting gives you the clearest, sharpest image of the three, offering a wide variety of typestyles and effects, including italics, bold letters, and justified margins. It is reproduced from photographic paper, the reason for its clarity. Typesetting is the preferred method, but it is also the most expensive.

If you have your resume typed, avoid models with cloth or nylon ribbons. Instead, be sure to have it done on an office-quality typewriter with a plastic (or carbon) ribbon. This can make an important difference in the way your resume appears.

We recommend word processors, which offer the most flexible approach. Resumes created on them can be modified easily and quickly, stored, and targeted to specific employers or job openings. Word processors have come a long way, and the major packages offer a wide variety of typefaces and styles in standard and proportional spacing. In fact, they're amazingly similar to typesetting. Word processing is a relatively inexpensive alternative, and this is what we use ourselves.

The next thing to consider is the choice of typeface. While you want your resume to stand out, you don't want it to compete with funeral or wedding announcements. Our advice is that you stick to a simple, clean typeface. There are, of course, thousands of typefaces from which to choose. However, we believe that those like English, Times Roman, or Helvetica are best because of their simplicity of design and clarity to the eye.

Another pitfall to avoid is combining different typeface styles (i.e., Times Roman and Helvetica). On the other hand, those *within* the same typeface family may be combined to produce an attractive visual effect. For example, Times Roman typefaces can come in light, light italic, medium, medium italic, bold, bold italic, and several other nuances.

Having chosen your typeface, it's time to lay out your resume. During the design phase, bear in mind that open spaces make your resume easier to read. Thus you should avoid cramming your page(s) with heavy masses of print. For example, take a look at Eleanora Unsura's two resumes in chapter five.

Finally, a word about printing those 25, 50, or 100 copies of the resume. If you have it typed, find and use the best quality offset printing process available. If you use a word processor, print as many originals as you need on attractive, letter-quality paper. Never send off photocopies of your resume to a potential employer. Photocopies are okay for friends or even employment agencies, but not the person with whom you want to win an interview.

Another point is that the resume you mail may be photocopied by a personnel department and subsequently passed along to other members of their firm. Copies made from copies can lose their readability In an emergency, some professionally-maintained office photocopiers may do a good job. We think it's better to avoid such emergencies by always having "perfect" copies of your resume on hand.

A final word; proofread your resume at every step in this process, whether it's typeset, typed, or generated from a word processor. Get a knowledgeable friend or colleague to help. Mistakes on resumes are embarrassing and unacceptable; they may prove disastrous. No matter how much you have paid to have your resume created, you're the one who loses if it isn't right. So be meticulous — don't settle for less than the very best.

Afterword

The infuriating truism that "everything is relative" can be — and often is — employed to defend the most eccentric, idiosyncratic, and at times, ill-conceived of practices and notions. In writing resumes, of course, what is bad and what is good depends upon what *works,* and what does not. Results are, in the final analysis, what count.

Certainly the element of chance may enter into landing a desirable position, as is true of every aspect of our lives. But a well-organized approach can minimize the random factors, and reduce the arbitrary flow of circumstances of which we may be unaware.

Our guidelines and suggestions are thus intended as a modest contribution in helping you increase your control over the factors governing a single aspect of your career: getting the interviews you want!

With this in mind, we've shown you the ingredients of successful resumes, with plenty of practical examples. Now you can recognize the difference between:

- Relevant vs. useless or potentially damaging information

- Active vs. static

- Attractive vs. unattractive

- Attention-getting vs. dull and unappealing

- Cover letters vs. personal sales letters

You know how to:

- Emphasize strengths and deemphasize weak
  nesses

- Focus on career objectives

- Write an interview-winning resume

Some things, perhaps, are relative, but effective resumes are based on the purpose and technique of a carefully conceived resume strategy. We hope that *The Resume Handbook* has given you the kind of strategy you'll need to help you get your foot in the door.

As we said before, the rest is up to you. Good luck!

ABOUT THE AUTHORS

Dave Hizer recently joined Right Associates of Farmington Hills, Michigan, which he describes as a "comprehensive human resources consulting firm," after nearly a decade with a "Fortune 50" bank, most recently as Director of Human Resources Planning.

With over 15 years experience creating and directing managerial and organizational development programs, this enterprising executive reads more resumes in a week than most people skim newspaper headlines in a month. He has authored numerous articles on career planning, self-marketing techniques and related topics, including "The ABC's of Cover Letters," which recently appeared in **The Wall Street Journal's** publication, **National Business Employment Weekly.**

The father of two energetic boys, Dave somehow finds the time to conduct national workshops and seminars on motivation, managerial leadership, career/ life planning, and the advantages of improved health consciousness on managerial performance.

Art Rosenberg is a New York/New Jersey-based technical consultant specializing in user-friendly documentation, corporate communications, and training. His recent publications include **Chess for Children and the Young at Heart** (Atheneum), a pair of studies on energy management systems (McGraw-Hill), and several journal articles, including "Making the Switch to a High-Tech Job" **(National Business Employment Weekly).**

Writer, inventor, lecturer, translator, and oenophile, this author is a former textbook acquisitions editor (Dun-Donnelley), marketing manager (McGraw-Hill), and international publisher (Harcourt Brace Jovanovich, and The United Nations in Geneva, Switzerland) who is partial to live opera, slow jazz, tournament chess, candlelight cuisine, good grammar, Monday Night Football, long science fiction novels, and short sentences (in no particular order).

NEW YORK! BOSTON! CHICAGO! CALIFORNIA! TEXAS! PENNSYLVANIA! WASHINGTON DC/BALTIMORE!

...and other major job markets!

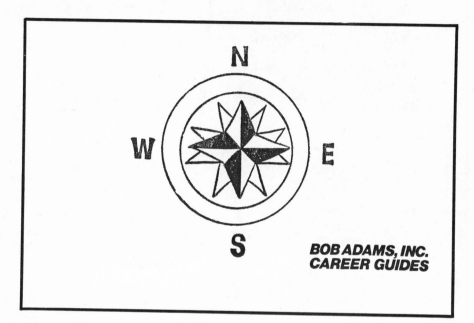

N

W

E

S

*BOB ADAMS, INC.
CAREER GUIDES*

CAREER PATHS   by the editors of Bob Adams, Inc.

More than 40 professionals who are pursuing diverse and exciting careers give first-person accounts of the ins and outs of their jobs: what they like and dislike about their chosen professions, how they got to where they are, and what they hope the future holds for them. Complementing these fascinating interviews are comprehensive sections on current salaries, industry outlooks for many diverse fields, and feature articles on the basics of job-hunting. "One of the best career books of the year ... We like this very much and if we had published the book, it would probably have been priced at $12.95."-**Career Opportunities News.** 248 pages, $7.95 paperback.

KNOCK 'EM DEAD   by Martin John Yate

Knock 'em Dead, written by the Director of Training for the Dunhill Personnel System, gives you not only the best answers to dozens of tough interview questions, but it also shows you the best way to answer. The interview is the most critical part of the job hunt, and the quality of every answer you give can mean the difference between a job offer and a rejection letter. **Knock 'em Dead** provides every interviewee with the edge necessary to anticipate the interviewer's questions and turn them into job offers. **Knock 'em Dead** not only tells you how to do well during the interview, but it also gives you practical advice on how to prepare for, and capture, the appointment. 156 pages, $5.95 paperback.

THE JOB BANK SERIES   by the editors of Bob Adams, Inc.

With 12 separate books covering major job markets throughout the United States, the **Job Bank** series continues to offer job hunters comprehensive and up-to-date information on major employers in each of the 12 regions covered. Readers will find the kind of critical information necessary to structure a successful job search: address and telephone number of each firm, contact names, a thorough description of the firm's primary business, professional positions commonly filled, educational backgrounds sought, and fringe benefits offered. Each of the 12 books also includes an industry cross-index, and complete sections on mounting a successful job-hunting campaign. **Job Bank** books are available for the following areas: Pennsylvania, Chicago, Washington DC, San Francisco/Bay Area, Boston, Texas, Southern California, Atlanta, the Southwest (CO, AZ, NM, UT), Ohio, the Northwest (WA, OR), and New York. 200-400 pages (depending on market size), all books $9.95 paperback.

Available at your local bookstore, or direct from the publisher. To order by mail, please include $1.75 per order to cover postage and handling.

BOB ADAMS, INC.
840 Summer Street, Boston MA 02127
617/268-9570

The Job Bank series gives you
AMERICA'S JOBS

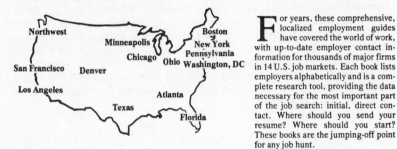

F or years, these comprehensive, localized employment guides have covered the world of work, with up-to-date employer contact information for thousands of major firms in 14 U.S. job markets. Each book lists employers alphabetically and is a complete research tool, providing the data necessary for the most important part of the job search: initial, direct contact. Where should you send your resume? Where should you start? These books are the jumping-off point for any job hunt.

An industry cross-index lets you pinpoint employers in your particular field, and helpful sections on the basics of job-winning, and resumes and cover letters, are powerful complements to the rest of your research.

Whether you have just graduated, decided to change careers, or simply decided to change employers, these local Job Bank books will steer you, your career, and your resume in the right direction.

Each Job Bank book shows you where, and to whom, to send your resume. Useful information on 500-1500 of the largest local employers includes:

- Address and telephone number
- Contact person's name and title
- Brief description of business activities
- Professional job categories*
- Educational backgrounds sought*
- Fringe benefits offered*
  *included in many, but not all, entries

Rush me the latest editions of these books from the Job Bank series ($9.95 each)!

- ___ Atlanta*
- ___ Boston
- ___ Greater Chicago
- ___ Denver*
- ___ Florida*
- ___ Greater Los Angeles
- ___ Minneapolis*
- ___ Metropolitan New York

- ___ Northwest
- ___ Ohio
- ___ Pennsylvania
- ___ San Francisco
- ___ Texas
- ___ Washington, DC*

*available April 1987

Also, rush me these other job-search books

- ___ Knock 'em Dead with Great Answers to Tough Interview Questions ($5.95)
- ___ The Resume Handbook ($5.95)
- ___ Career Paths: An Exploration of Career Options ($7.95)
- ___ A Guide to Becoming a Flight Attendant ($6.95)
- ___ Careers and the College Grad ($12.95)
- ___ Careers and the MBA ($14.95)
- ___ The National Job Bank (50 states: $129.95)
- ___ The Job Bank Guide to Employment Services (50 states: $99.95)

Please add $1.75 for shipping and handling to your order. Use your credit card to order by telephone, or send your check or money order to:

Name: _____

Address: _____

City/State/Zip: _____

BOB ADAMS, INC.
CAREER GUIDES

840 Summer St.
Boston, MA 02127

CALL TOLL-FREE 1-800-USA-JOBS
(In Massachusetts call 617/268-9570)